ANGELS REALLY DO EXIST

SIGNS OF HEAVEN ON EARTH

DAVID O. DYKES

For a complete list of resources and broadcast messages by Dr. David O. Dykes, visit:
www.gabc.org

Green Acres Baptist Church
1607 Troup Highway
Tyler, Texas 75701
www.gabc.org

Produced with the assistance of Fluency Organization, Inc. in Tyler, TX. Cover design by DK Designs Group.

By David O. Dykes:

Jesus Storyteller: Timeless Truths from His Parables

Revelation: God's Final Word

No, That's Not in the Bible

ALSO BY DAVID O. DYKES:

Finding Peace in Your Pain

Ten Requirements for America's Survival

Character Out of Chaos

Handling Life's Disappointments

Do Angels Really Exist?

Check for e-reader availability of books:

Table of Contents

CHAPTER ONE

Recognizing Heaven on Earth

It was as close to heaven as she'd ever been. A young teenage girl from South Texas and her friends enjoyed a summer afternoon of swimming at a church camp's lake property in North Carolina. The lake stretched out six acres in size and its calm, glassy surface reflected the mountains and sky. Accustomed to the hurried traffic and looming skyscrapers of her metropolitan hometown, the young girl would later recall thinking at the time, "It was as close to heaven as I had been." She just didn't know how true her words would prove to be.

Each day, she and her friends became more daring in their swimming ventures into the cold, deep waters. Not a particularly good swimmer, she ordinarily didn't swim where she couldn't touch or see the bottom. Nevertheless, on this day, she was feeling exhilarated by the icy cold mountain water and soon floated and dog-paddled out into the middle of the lake.

As she lay on her back floating gently along and gazing at the clouds overhead, a sudden cramp in her left leg seized her body with pain. She instantly doubled up to rub the knots of muscle in her lower leg. Distracted by her injury, she slowly began sinking into the water. Fear gripped her the moment she realized she could no longer feel the bottom of the lake.

She flailed her arms, swallowing a mouthful of water with every stroke. Panicked, she looked around for someone close by—a friend or one of her counselors—to help. No one was near and it appeared the lifeguard couldn't see her. As the water rushed in, burning her nose and throat, she finally managed to blurt out, "Oh, God, help me!"

Instantly, a man swam up from behind her and calmly said, "Put your hand on my shoulder." Without touching her, he issued the simple command in a reassuring voice that remains lodged in her memory to this day. She remembers noticing his pale skin, blue eyes and light red hair, but little else about him. She willingly clung to his shoulder as he silently swam toward shore.

In the distance, the camp lifeguard waited at the pier with a large towel to receive the frightened girl. She climbed the wooden ladder, shaking and shivering, and wrapped up in the towel to get warm. Turning to thank the kind man who rescued her, she saw he was gone. When she asked the lifeguard about her rescuer, the puzzled woman explained there was no such man.

For several minutes, the breathless young girl argued that a redheaded man had saved her life and helped her to the pier. Didn't anyone see what had happened? Still, the lifeguard kept insisting the young girl had come sputtering and splashing to the pier on her own. Finally, realizing that she wasn't going to change the lifeguard's mind (or vice versa), the young girl thanked her for her help and started toward her cabin.

Brushing back tears, the girl went over the terrifying incident in her mind the rest of the afternoon. "I realized the man had looked different and had spoken very calmly," she recalls. "Instead of reaching for me, he had told me what to do. Why was the lifeguard unable to see him and where did he go after he saw me safely delivered?"[1]

Is Seeing Believing?

In a world accustomed to believing only what we can see with our eyes, the idea that invisible, spiritual beings exist all around us is unnerving to many. Yet the history and folklore of every culture mentions some form of "spirits," confirming the universal suspicion that we're not alone.

Webster's Dictionary defines the supernatural as: "of or relating to an order of existence beyond the visible observable universe." In other words, there's more going on around us than we can see with our limited vision. Indeed, the young girl in this story did, in fact, experience "heaven on earth"—not only the breathtaking beauty of the Carolinas, but the red-haired variety of heaven on earth in the form of a mysterious, life-saving angel.

It would be the pinnacle of presumption for us to think we're the only beings in God's creation. We're *human* beings, but the Bible teaches that there's also an innumerable host of *heavenly* beings.

Maybe you remember the classic bar scene from the first *Star Wars* movie. On the remote planet of Tatooine, Luke Skywalker and Obi-Wan Kenobi enter a futuristic cantina, catering to a startling array of outlandish creatures. Inside, they're living it up and enjoying funky big band music in the background. From bubble-headed and multi-eyed to long-snouted and furry, they're just the kind of out-of-this-world patrons one might expect to see in a galactic bar. It's life as usual on Tatooine, but the human patrons look extremely out of place among this odd menagerie.

It's not quite that far out, but the Bible also describes a fantastic variety of God's heavenly beings. In heaven, life as usual involves heavenly creatures continually worshiping around the throne: seraphim, cherubim and an entire order of spirit beings. We'll explore later what we know about this order of beings, but for now I just want to call your attention to the fact that there's an entire invisible world, populated by heavenly creatures we cannot see.

In this realm, we're often more like Luke and Obi-Wan in unfamiliar and even uncomfortable territory. However, if you're a *Star Wars* fan, you know some of the stranger creatures from Tatooine become central characters in the plot, not to mention compadres with Luke Skywalker.

The more time he spent with them, learning about and from them, the less strange they seemed. In the same way, I want to challenge you to spend some time pondering the invisible world of spiritual beings. Thinking this way will bring you a new perspective about everyday life as you learn to recognize the signs of heaven on earth all around you.

It's like a movie director investigating a location for a particular film scene. He often positions his hands up, with his thumbs touching, to make a model of a "screen." He frames whatever image he wants inside that box and keeps the audience from seeing anything else around it. The director obviously doesn't want us to see the camera, lights, pieces of the set or the assistants holding microphones.

However, we've all watched B-movies where a microphone accidentally slips in from the top of the screen. You may have seen Westerns with power lines mysteriously stretching across the background! Something like that serves as a reminder that what we see on the television or movie screen is only a sliver of reality. There's much more going on behind the scenes.

The same is true of this world. The Bible says, "So we fix our eyes not on what is seen, but on what is unseen. For what is seen is temporary, but what is unseen is eternal" (2 Corinthians 4:18). We can only see a small slice of what's real. Meanwhile, an entire world of spiritual activity is going on around us. Occasionally, God allows a heavenly "microphone" or spiritual "power line" to slip into the screen to remind us of that fact. That explains the occasional appearance of angels and reminds us of their continual, unseen activity in our lives.

Angels in Pop Culture

Spiritual beings and unseen mysteries fascinate us. Hollywood and human imagination have given us many strange ideas about these spirit beings: who they are, where they reside and what they do. Although these popular beliefs are often more fiction than truth, the entertainment industry leads the way in creatively capitalizing on our society's intrigue with the supernatural.

Today, Hollywood's most popular scripts interweave the unknown and the unseen. The supernatural also fuels the plots of much of our modern television programming and has boosted sales in the electronic gaming industry. Long gone are the days of Pac Man and Asteroids; today's young people do battle on their computer screens with electronic recreations of spirits, demons and the spiritual forces of good and evil.

In the 1990s, the television series *Touched by an Angel* was unique in its market, featuring the encounters between angels and troubled humans. However, today's television lineup often showcases the supernatural. For example, a drama about a woman who "communicates" with murder victims in order solve crimes had more than 13 million viewers in its first season. Most of the major networks have one or more primetime shows with a supernatural element to it. The supernatural is getting a lot of press these days.

Two Extremes

When it comes to the subject of angels, people seem to be divided into two extremes. On one hand, most people, including Christians, seem to be ignorant about the facts. On the other hand, a growing number of people are becoming obsessed with the topic. In either case, there's no shortage of information available. Angels started becoming a trendy fad in our consumer-driven culture over a dozen years ago, and our fascination has now broadened into an unhealthy interest in all things supernatural, including the paranormal.

Walk into any bookstore and you'll find more angel books written from a secular perspective than from a biblical viewpoint. For example, we could consult more than 15,000 books categorized under "Angels" on a popular online bookstore.[2] The topics range from learning to communicate with your angel, to experiencing healing through angels.

Is Ignorance Bliss?

Which of these two categories do you fit into—ignorance or obsession? I confess that for much of my Christian life I was totally clueless regarding what the Bible teaches about angels. And I grew up in a wonderful, Bible-preaching church! I went to Sunday school and to worship services twice a week, but I can't recall hearing a single lesson or sermon about angels.

When I was older, I went to a Christian university where I majored in religion. Yet, I can't recall any of my professors teaching about angels. After college, I completed seven years of post-graduate work in one of the most respected seminaries in America. How many lectures or lessons about angels did I receive there? Zilch. Nada. Zero.

Several years ago, I even consulted my textbooks on systematic theology, only to find that angels weren't even listed in the index! And yet, there are several passages in the Bible about angels, and we'll look at many of them in this book. I'm not the kind to develop a conspiracy complex, but perhaps there's a cunning satanic strategy to keep God's people (and others) in the dark about the wonderful subject of angels. (Sadly, many of God's people are blissfully ignorant on a wide variety of biblical truths.)

When I discovered how little scriptural information on angels was available, I began an in-depth study on the topic. I started by reading every passage in the Bible that mentioned angels. Thanks to the modern convenience of Bible software programs, that was the easy part. I quickly searched for every occurrence of the words "angels, spirits, cherubs, seraphs," etc. I wasn't prepared for the number of passages I discovered. I soon printed a thick stack of single-spaced pages containing hundreds of them.

Obviously, I wasn't aware the Bible had *that* much to say about angels. However, I was convicted that if God's Word devoted that much attention to angels, I should be more informed. Maybe you feel the same way, too. I believe followers of Christ should strive to learn what the Bible says about every blessing God has for us. So, if you're ignorant about angels (as I once was), I pray you'll have a hunger and thirst to learn the truth.

An Unhealthy Obsession

While many people are in the dark about angels, others are so fascinated and enchanted by the topic that their interest borders on an unhealthy obsession. Interest in angels isn't confined to Christians; millions of Americans are literally entranced by angels.

Most secular sources have communicated many misconceptions about angels and the spiritual realm in general. For example, what was recognized in the '80s and '90s as the New Age religion was actually the same old mystical Eastern religion, just dressed in California clothes!

With their touchy-feely, anything-goes attitude, New Agers stepped over the line of truth and talked about getting in touch with their "inner angel." Along with one of their highly visible Hollywood adherents, they claimed to hear words of instruction from their "channeling spirits" (unwittingly opening themselves up to demonic activity). Today, the term "New Age" has diversified under a more culturally relevant umbrella of "alternative faith communities," and the movement itself has gained speed.

Nevertheless, the same false teaching continues to confuse many people, including Christians, leading some into spiritism and the use of mediums, believing they can communicate with their dear, departed loved ones. This practice is not only deceptive, it's dangerous. In the 21st century, we've seen this practice go mainstream. Case in point: a recent daytime television show featured a host who would "read" different audience members to connect them with the departed souls he says communicate with him.

In addition to the entertainment industry, there's great commercial interest in the spiritual dimension. Angels are big business these days. In many malls and stores across America, one can peruse an endless selection of angel pins, angel pictures, angel clothes and angel books. Those who prefer to shop in their slippers can go online to any number of angel merchants, including more than 1,300 listings related to jewelry, watches and angel collectibles on one site alone.[3]

However, angel worship is nothing new. In fact, the Bible specifically warned people in the first century A.D. against it. "Do not let anyone who delights in false humility *and the worship of angels* [emphasis added] disqualify you for the prize. Such a person goes into great detail about what he has seen, and his unspiritual mind puffs him up with idle notions" (Colossians 2:18). Although I believe there's much for us to learn about angels and recognizing heaven on earth, we must keep our focus on Jesus Christ, not His holy angels.

Why This Book?

So, why are you reading this book? It's a fair question. After all, something must have piqued your interest in this title. Your answer may reveal the most about your present response to angels. Are you interested in the supernatural perhaps to an unhealthy degree? Or are you largely ignorant of the biblical facts about the spiritual dimension of reality?

As with many spiritual issues, we find God's truth balanced between the extremes. (Of course, there are other responses we'll examine later that are actually worse than either extreme.) We shouldn't be ignorant about angels, but we must also guard against becoming enamored with them.

The Superiority of Jesus

Of all the biblical references about angels, we find the most instructive words in Hebrews 1:13. The Holy Spirit inspired the writer of Hebrews to expose the superiority of Jesus over anything in existence. The treatise discusses how Jesus is superior to angels, to Moses, to the Law and to the Old Testament sacrificial system.

In his development of how Jesus is superior to angels, we find this gem of truth in Hebrews 1:13-14: "To which of the angels did God ever say, 'Sit at my right hand until I make your enemies a footstool for your feet?' Are not all angels ministering spirits sent to serve those who will inherit salvation?"

This concise statement reveals both the identity and purpose of angels and helps us avoid the extremes of ignorance or obsession. Angels are so much more than porcelain figures or golden lapel pins. They are special spirits sent to serve God's children. Hebrews identifies them as "spirits"—that means they are "spirit beings" who are not confined to the limitations of "human beings."

This verse also defines their purpose. They are "sent to serve those who will inherit salvation" (the saints). So a simple, alliterative statement regarding what the Bible teaches about angels is: Angels are Spirits Sent to Serve the

Saints. Out of His gracious concern for us, our Father sends His angels to assist us.

Angel Neglect

You might not be obsessed or ignorant regarding angels. However, perhaps you may have been guilty of another response altogether—neglecting the reality of angels and the spiritual dimension of our world. Are you generally unaware of all God's Word says about the ministry of God's mighty angels? Have you ever been guilty of expressing disbelief about angels? Perhaps you still categorize angels with elves, fairies and other mythical creatures.

I've noticed that when a person starts talking about angels, many non-Christians will look at him or her as if that individual is "off the wall." Unfortunately, some Christians react with similar alarm. We must remember that Jesus Christ Himself taught about and recognized the existence of angels. Jesus also had personal encounters with angels on many occasions while on earth. To discount the reality of angels is to doubt what Jesus Christ said about them.

Jesus emphasized that angels are actively engaged in our world, traveling back and forth to heaven. In the first chapter of John's gospel, Jesus surprises Nathanael by revealing that He supernaturally saw him sitting alone under a fig tree. When Nathanael responds with amazement that Jesus knew where he had just been, Jesus replies, "You believe because I told you I saw you under the fig tree. You shall see greater things than that. I tell you the truth, you shall see heaven open, and the angels of God ascending and descending on the Son of Man" (John 1:50–51).

If God suddenly opened our spiritual eyes, I believe we'd see a steady stream of angels traveling to and from heaven. It seems some angels are "on active duty" on earth at times, and then are relieved by other angels, at which time they get to return to heaven for a little "R and R" (revelation and rejoicing). Jacob observed the same vision Jesus described. In Jacob's dream, he saw a stairway into heaven with angels ascending and descending (Genesis 28:12).

As we study this interesting topic, one of my goals is that you'll come to appreciate the fact that the Bible teaches the spiritual dimension is just as real as the world we see with our physical eyes. We don't often see as well with our "eyes of faith" in our material, seeing-is-believing modern culture. Nevertheless, I hope you'll keep an open mind and begin looking for evidence of heaven on earth going on around you.

Angel Apathy

Perhaps the worst response to the spiritual dimension and heavenly beings isn't ignorance, obsession or neglect; it's apathy. Could it be that while you believe in the reality of angels, you just don't care? It just doesn't seem to make a difference in your everyday life—you're so caught up in *this* world that you rarely give thought to the greater spiritual world that coexists alongside of it? If that is your current attitude, you have the most to gain from this study of angels. God has provided these wonderful, ministering spirits to help us as believers. Ask God right now to open your mind and your heart to the presence and activity of angels around you.[4]

Fact vs. Fantasy

How much of what we're hearing about angelic activity is factual and how much is fantasy? Borrowing from one of the mottos of the Reformation, "Sola Scriptura" (translated, "Scripture Alone") must be the baseline of our research into angels. When it comes to understanding the truth about angels and spiritual reality, we must turn to the Bible. Because there's so much false teaching about angels, it's imperative that we limit our beliefs to what we find in Scripture, and Scripture alone.

So, what does the Bible say about angels? The following short quiz might surprise you and even unsettle what you think you already know about angels. (Don't worry; no one will know how you did on the quiz but you!) Read through each question and choose your answer carefully.

How Much Do You Know about Angels?

1. All of God's angels have wings.

    True False

2. The total number of angels who are specifically named in the Bible is:

    a. Four

    b. Three

    c. Seven

    d. Two

3. For extra credit, what are the names of the angels the Bible specifically cites?

4. What is the total number of the heavenly host?

    a. 144,000

    b. 7,000

    c. Over 1 million

    d. No one knows

5. Most angels are good human beings who have died and gone to heaven.

   True False

6. According to the Bible, angels most often appear:

   a. As ordinary men

   b. As winged heavenly creatures

   c. As chubby-cheeked babies

   d. Singing spiritual beings with harps

   e. B and A

7. Satan was once God's special angel.
   True False

8. According to the Bible, which of the following tasks and/or messages were carried out by angels? Choose all that apply.

   a. Important birth announcements

   b. God's judgment against disobedient nations

   c. Proclaiming the gospel message of salvation

   d. Encouragement

   e. Enforcing a deadly plague

f. Striking an evil king dead

g. Fixing a meal

9. How many times does the Bible record angels singing?

a. At the birth of Jesus.

b. After Jesus was resurrected from the dead.

c. At the throne of God in heaven.

d. Both A and C.

e. None of the above.

10. To signal Jesus' return to earth, which angel will blow a trumpet?

a. Michael

b. Gabriel

c. The Bible doesn't say.

Now, check your answers:

1. False

2. B

3. Michael, Gabriel, Lucifer

4. D

5. False

6. E

7. True

8. All except C

9. E (Don't believe it? Keep reading!)

10. C

Score Your Answers:

1-3 Correct—You may not know the difference between angels and "angles."

4-6 Correct—Congratulations, you're about average.

7-9 Correct—You've read this book before!

10 Correct—You may be an angel in disguise.

How did you do? Even if you did well, I hope this quiz has aroused your curiosity to learn more about the Bible says (and doesn't say) about angels.

In fact, if you want to get the most out of this study, I encourage you to set aside everything you've ever heard about angels. Then, as we examine God's Word, you can begin to reconstruct a true biblical image of God's special, supernatural helpers. A careful study of what the Bible says about the spiritual realm and the angels who inhabit it will remove the confusing mystery and open our lives to the wonderful ministry of angels.

---

[1] Based on a personal account as told by Marsha Head.

[2] At the time of this writing, amazon.com lists more than 15,000 books related to angels.

[3] At the time of this writing, amazon.com lists more than 1,300 merchandise items related to angels.

[4] I encourage you to read Frank Peretti's first two novels, *This Present Darkness* and *Piercing the Darkness*. These excellent works of fiction are based on the truth of invisible spiritual warfare going on around us. I think you'll find the books to be very good reading, and your eyes will be opened to a whole new world of the role of God's mighty angels.

CHAPTER TWO

Just the FAQs

Like any other young man who grew up in a small town, he dreamed of making a life for himself far away from home. Maybe he'd become a well-respected lawyer, a surgeon who saved lives or even a successful international businessman. More than anything, he wanted to leave his mark on the world. However, following in his father's footsteps, the family business and small-town responsibilities destined him to live a life of humble anonymity. He would never even leave the city limits.

After struggling financially for awhile to keep the family business afloat, the pressure continued to mount until one night he concluded his seemingly meaningless life wasn't worth living anymore. He checked out of the office and decided to check out of life. Thankfully, the voice of a stranger interrupted his plans—a divine encounter that changed his life and showed him what the world would be like had he never been born.

Each Christmas, I watch the Frank Capra movie, *It's a Wonderful Life.* It's one of the most popular movies of all time. Jimmy Stewart plays George Bailey, a good man in small-town Bedford Falls who inherits his father's business and soon finds himself in deep financial trouble. In the depth of his depression, George stands on a snow-covered bridge looking toward the dark water below. He has decided to jump into the icy water and take his life, so his family can benefit from his life insurance policy.

At precisely that moment, George sees another man jump into the water. George's goodness compels him to jump in to rescue the man, who turns out to be George's bumbling guardian angel named Clarence, played by Henry Travers. Clarence is sent from heaven to show George what life would have been like if he had never been born, and to convince him his life is indeed worth living.

Clarence identifies himself as a man who died in the 1800s who's been working for years to "earn his wings" and graduate from second-class angel status. If he succeeds in helping George, he can earn his wings and become an "angel first-class."

At the climax of the movie, the citizens of Bedford Falls, grateful for all of George's selfless acts through the years, bring in money to help him pay off his debts. Everyone is singing and rejoicing as George embraces his little daughter Zuzu. Suddenly, they hear a bell on their Christmas tree tinkle. That's Zuzu's cue to say her classic line, "Teacher says, 'Every time a bell rings, an angel gets his wings.'" George looks up with a smile and says, "That a boy, Clarence!"

It makes a great Christmas tradition, but how close is it to the truth about angels? Unfortunately, this is a typical example of how Hollywood unintentionally promotes false teachings about angels. That movie is just one of dozens that promote the idea that human beings become angels after they die.

When I'm searching for the truth about any issue, I look first in the Bible. Where the Bible speaks, I speak with certainty. Where the Bible is silent, I'm silent. To find the truth about angels, we must open our hearts to believe what God's Word says, not what we read or hear in the secular media.

Nor can we always believe what an individual says happened to him or her concerning an angel encounter. Unless the experience coincides with what God's Word says about angels, it's suspect at best. God's Word helps us separate the fantasy from the facts. Let's examine some of the more popular fantasies about angels and compare and contrast them to the biblical facts—starting with our dear "angel" friend Clarence.

Are Angels Human Beings Who Have Died?

The fantasy: Angels are human beings who have died. **The biblical fact:** Angels are spiritual beings created by God.

Where did we get the notion that angels are human beings who have died, gone to heaven and acquired wings? Folk tales, popular fiction and the movies have promoted the idea for years, until it has become almost universally accepted as truth. Sometimes, even well-meaning Christians will say something that reflects this fantasy. When a loved one dies, they may attempt to comfort themselves by saying, "Well, God has another angel," or something to that effect.

We know they mean their loved one is in heaven, but God doesn't really have another angel in that person. If the deceased was a Christian, God has another saint who has died and gone to heaven. The idea of loved ones dying and becoming angels isn't taught in Scripture. Angels are *not* human beings who have died. Angels are unique spiritual beings created at the beginning of time.

You may have read so-called "angel stories" that promote this fantasy. For example, a person might say, "I had an encounter with an angel who turned out to be my Aunt Gertrude who passed away twelve years ago." You can be sure that when the so-called angel is someone the speaker recognizes, it's either a deceiving spirit or the person is deceiving himself or herself. There's not a single verse in the Bible that even suggests a person can become an angel after he or she dies.

Well, then, what *does* the Bible teach about angels? Colossians 1:16 tells us Jesus created everything. "For by him all things were created: things in heaven and on earth, visible and invisible, whether thrones or powers or rulers or authorities; all things were created by him and for him." The angels are those "invisible" things Jesus created—uniquely different from human creation on many levels.

Humans Differ from Angels

The Bible distinguishes humans from angels on a number of levels. For example, angels never age in the Bible. There's no scriptural evidence of an angel dying, or even being born. There are no "baby angels" or "geriatric angels." In fact, Jesus taught that angels do not experience a marital relationship that produces offspring.

In Mark 12, some religious leaders with misgivings about life after death asked Jesus a loaded question. These Sadducees set up a sarcastic scenario about a woman who had been married seven times, and then asked Jesus: "At the resurrection whose wife will she be, since the seven were married to her?" (Mark 12:23).

Instead of this farfetched riddle insulting Him, Jesus uses it as an opportunity to teach us something about our resurrection condition and about angels.

Jesus replied, "When the dead rise, they will neither marry nor be given in marriage; they will be like the angels in heaven" (Mark 12:25). Before you can understand the truth of this amazing statement, you must first comprehend what Jesus is *not* saying. First, He isn't saying we become angels when we die. He says we *are like angels* in respect to the new relationships we'll have in heaven.

Second, Jesus isn't saying we won't maintain the knowledge of our spouses when we get to heaven. He's simply saying there'll be no *new* marriages at that time. In heaven, there'll be no wedding bells for human weddings.

In fact, we never read in the Bible of female angels. Examples of angels always appear in the Bible as men. God created the first woman, Eve, as a necessary companion and helper to Adam, the first man. Apparently, angels don't share the same human need for companionship and marriage.

Some believe this passage teaches that angels are sexless or without gender. That may be stretching the truth because, in Genesis 19, two angels entered Sodom and the wicked men of Sodom wanted to have sex with them (Genesis 19:4-5). The Bible doesn't say if this was even a possibility, but at least it appeared to those Sodomites that it was possible.

Another fascinating scriptural passage related to this is Genesis 6:1-4. This speaks of "sons of God" who had sexual relations with women before the flood. The result was a race of giants called "Nephilim." Some commentators believe these were angels and tie this event with Jude 6, which speaks of angels who did not "keep their position" and are chained in darkness for future judgment. (Don't study these passages unless you want to spend a lot of time scratching your head.)

This gets really confusing, and it's impossible to make a dogmatic conclusion from these passages. However, we're safe to insist that angels do not marry one another. Some husbands today may insist that "I married an angel," but an angel himself will never make that claim.

Angels Do Not Die

Except for the generation of Christians who are still alive when Jesus returns, we'll all die because we're human. "Man is destined to die once, and after that to face judgment" (Hebrews 9:27).

After He addresses the marriage issue in heaven, Jesus continues His focus on what it will be like after we die by noting: "and they [Christians] can no longer die; for they are like the angels" (Luke 20:36). Once a Christian has physically died, he or she won't ever die again. (A nonbeliever will suffer the "second death," according to Revelation 20:14, which is a spiritual death—eternal separation from God.)

Search the Scriptures to discover the death of an angel. It's not there. Physical death in a person results from sickness, injury or simply old age. The Bible never speaks of an angel getting sick or injured. It seems as if Jesus is teaching that angels never age or die—they are eternal spiritual beings. It's wonderful to realize that one day we'll be like the angels in this respect.

On the basis of God's Word, we can conclude that the angels are immortal spiritual beings created by God and uniquely different from humans. Free your mind from the fantasy that they're loved ones who died and are trying to "earn" their wings.

What Do Angels Look Like?

The fantasy: Angels appear as chubby babies with wings. **The biblical fact:** Angels most often appear as ordinary men.

This fantasy, conceived in the fertile minds of creative artists and storytellers, portrays angels as chubby infants with wings. Angels are frequently depicted in paintings, books and films as cupid-like, wing-bearing babies who shoot romantic arrows into the hearts of lovers. Many people love collecting these angel figurines. My wife does, too. There's nothing wrong with enjoying these decorative objects.

However, I have a feeling that when we finally get to meet God's angels, we'll likely be shocked at how the ceramic figurines and artists' depictions fall short of portraying God's mighty angels. We may fantasize that angels are rosy-cheeked babies with little wings and halos, but the facts, according to the Bible, are that they usually appear as ordinary men.

The adjective "ordinary" really doesn't apply because angels are truly extraordinary, so for lack of a better term we'll refer to the broad category of angels as "God's holy angels." The Bible never portrays this larger group of angels as having wings. However, a unique category of angels called seraphim and cherubim do, in fact, have wings. We'll look at these special angels later in our study.

However, for the sake of our current discussion, the mere fact that God's holy angels are most often described as appearing as men would seem to confirm that they don't have wings. Recall Jacob's dream in Genesis 28:12 in which he saw angels climbing a ladder or stairway back and forth into heaven. It seems logical that if they had wings, they wouldn't need a ladder!

The idea of winged supernatural beings is rooted in many pagan religions. They often featured winged gods or servants of the gods who made somewhat angelic, sudden appearances and delivered important messages. Consider Mercury, the messenger of the Roman gods with wings attached to his ankles (and the fleet-footed symbol of a popular flower delivery company). An internationally known athletic-wear manufacturer shares its name with *Nike* (the Greek goddess of victory), a winged woman who looks a lot like the angelic figurines we see today. Winged supernatural beings were a staple of pagan religions.

Angels in Art

In fact, early Christian artists often avoided portraying angels in their work, in an effort to distinguish the newly founded Christianity from longstanding pagan religions in and around the Roman Empire.[1] After the rule of Constantine and the firm establishment of Christianity in the fourth century A.D., angels then began to surface as a central theme in Christian art.[2]

During the Renaissance, Italian artists popularized the winged cherub-faced babies (referred to as "putti") often seen today casting adoring glances on the front of Valentine's Day cards and other collectibles. The Renaissance period also produced some of the most memorable and beautiful portrayals of angels, from Leonardo da Vinci's small *Annunciation*, which is housed in the Louvre, to Sandro Botticelli's angelic detail in *The Coronation of the Virgin*.

The Italian artist, Raffaello Sanzio (better known as Raphael), reached the pinnacle of artistic expression of angels as sweet-faced babies. He copied his hyperbolic painting style from Michelangelo, who painted the famous scene on the ceiling of the Sistine Chapel. Throughout the centuries, most artists' angel portrayals have been of winged creatures, primarily female in gender, despite the fact that the Bible portrays angels appearing as just the opposite.

In fact, in many angel encounters in the Old Testament, angels are mistaken for men. When Abraham encountered three angels, they appeared as three strangers. He actually mistook them for men and offered them a meal (Genesis 18:2). When Manoah, who was the father-to-be of Samson, encountered an angel, he thought it was merely a man. He didn't realize until later that it was an angel (Judges 13:21).

Throughout the Bible, we read of angels simply appearing as mortals. The only clues that give them away as angels is by the divine message they deliver (Acts 1:10); or often, they're described as having faces or clothes that shine (Matthew 28:3). This brightness seems to be representative of their character. According to the Bible, the angel outside Jesus' tomb donned clothes as white as snow, whiter than any modern detergent could ever get them.

If I've convinced you that the majority of God's angels don't have wings, I hope I can also alter the picture you have in your mind's eye of angels with halos. While angels do seem to exude a glorious brightness, there's no biblical evidence that they have bands of light encircling their heads. Have you ever wondered why in artistic depictions (and church Christmas pageants) angels are often seen with halos? A halo is descriptive of the kind of glory these heavenly beings possess.

Designating deity, saints, angels and other important cultural figures with a halo symbol (also called a "nimbus") can be traced throughout the ages, including Roman, Greek and Egyptian culture. For example, depictions of Roman emperors often portrayed their power with a circle or band of radiant light. For hundreds of years, early Christian artists depicted Christ, the angels and even the apostles with similar halos.

However, during the Renaissance, the halo seems to have lost its popularity with mainstream Renaissance artists. Compare most early depictions of Christ with the depiction of Leonardo's da Vinci's famous *Last Supper* painting and you'll notice da Vinci omitted halos altogether and conveyed the glory of Christ through His central position at the table, His facial expression and other details.[3]

Although the Bible describes God as "light" and makes several references to the bright and glorious presence of God, the specific halo symbol is man-made, not necessarily biblical in origin.

Was It an Angel?

There have been several occasions in my life where I suspect I was assisted by an angelic minister, and I haven't seen any wings yet! One of these encounters involved some "supernatural assistance" I received at an airport in Moscow, Russia.

In the summer of 1993, I was leading a group of thirty-six volunteer missionaries from our church into the former

Soviet Union to conduct concerts in the Russian language, pass out Russian Bibles and do other evangelistic work.

I'll never forget the faces of the Russian men and women who packed a large civic center at one of our concerts—many of whom had never heard the gospel message. God blessed us in a tremendous way, with more than two thousand people responding to God's offer of love and forgiveness.

The most difficult part of the entire trip was coordinating our travel and transportation arrangements. Staying in Moscow and using the Vnukovo (domestic) Airport is a genuine nightmare. This airport is old-fashioned, dark and terribly inefficient. On our way through Moscow to the Crimea, it took us several hours to get processed.

On our return trip, we were facing a real challenge, because we only had a short time to claim our luggage and take a bus from the Vnukovo Airport to transfer to the Sheremetyevo International Airport, about 30 miles away. Anyone who has visited the former Soviet Union can understand our predicament.

The Russians never seem to be in a hurry and, in fact, they often have an aversion to doing things efficiently. We were late arriving at Vnukovo, so we retrieved our luggage and boarded the bus as quickly as we could. We were about an hour late when we arrived at Sheremetyevo, and our flight was scheduled to leave within an hour.

We quickly unloaded our bus and entered the crowded, confusing scene of the massive airport. All countries have a customs inspection point for arriving passengers, but when you're *leaving* Russia, passengers are required to go through a customs inspection, in case someone is trying to smuggle out antiquities.

As we looked at the long line waiting to go through the inspection, we realized it would take at least two hours, so it was clear we wouldn't make our flight. No one in our group looked forward to the prospect of missing our flight back to America, and I quickly began to pray for God's help.

Imagine the scene: thirty-six bone-tired Americans, loaded down with luggage, standing in an endless line in a place where none of us spoke fluent Russian. We were pretty discouraged, when a middle-aged man in blue coveralls approached me and said in fairly decent English, "May I help you?" To our group, he appeared to be an airport employee.

I breathed a prayer of thanks to God and explained to him that we were on a tight schedule, trying to make a Lufthansa flight to Frankfurt, Germany. He smiled and said, "No problem. Please have your group follow me."

Our convoy of people and luggage eagerly moved beside the long line of people and arrived at the place where customs agents were tediously checking the luggage of everyone leaving Russia. They were taking so much time to inspect each suitcase that I realized that even if they put us in the front of the line, most of the group wouldn't be finished by the time our flight departed.

Still, I was pleasantly surprised when our friend in the blue coveralls invited me to bring my group down to the far end of the customs area. There he enlisted another customs agent, just for our group. Miraculously, our group was cleared through with very little problem, and with only a few suitcases examined.

From there, each member of our group simply had to carry his or her luggage about fifty feet to the Lufthansa check-in. Everyone received boarding passes and, because the flight was already boarding, proceeded straight onto the plane.

Our friend in the blue coveralls was extremely helpful, and even made several trips to the check-in area for carry-on luggage for our group members. He was pleasant and friendly, and everyone commented on his kindness and help.

I'd already decided to give him a large tip for his help. So, after I made sure all our group had boarded, and that all the luggage would make the flight, I looked around to find our mysterious friend. He had brought my suitcase up to the counter only moments before, but now he was nowhere in sight.

It was as if he had simply disappeared. It was a large open area, and impossible to find a hiding place. I even walked all around the customs inspection and check-in area, but I never saw him again.

I approached the officer in charge of the customs inspection, who happened to be able to speak a few words of English. I carefully explained to him about the man who had helped us and that I wanted to show our appreciation to him. The inspection officer looked at me with a puzzled expression and said he knew of no one matching that description who worked at the airport. In fact, he said none of their employees wore blue coveralls!

I walked back to the check-in area, shaking my head, wondering if God had provided a special "airport angel" to assist our group. To this day, I strongly suspect that this ordinary looking man was God's special servant, sent to help His missionaries make it back to America on time.

Truth and Error

So far, we've learned that we're just as unlikely to receive an invitation to an "angel wedding" as we are to attend an "angel funeral," because angels are uniquely different from humans in so many ways. I've devoted much of this chapter to overcoming this fallacy that confuses angels with deceased human beings, because it's so strongly rooted in our culture today. In the next chapter, we'll take a look at even more FAQs—frequently asked questions—concerning truth and error when it comes to angels.

---

[1] Editors, *Christian History Magazine*, June 14, 2002, Christianity Today, Inc. Adapted from *New Advent, Catholic Encyclopedia*, 2004.

[2] The oldest existing examples of winged angels are represented in bas-reliefs of Carthage and a representation on ivory of St. Michael (on display in the British Museum) from the fourth century.

[3] Over the years, I've developed a personal interest in and appreciation for Renaissance art. Two excellent resources for Renaissance art are *The Renaissance Art Book*, by Wanda O'Reilly et.al; and *Renaissance Art: A Crash Course*, by David Boyle.

CHAPTER THREE

Just the FAQs—Part 2

Have you ever noticed how a proud new mother will look into the face of her newborn baby and say, "Oh, what a sweet little angel?" (Of course, parents don't usually say that when the child hits three or four!) Babies are cute, but to call them angels is yet another misunderstanding of the Bible's description of angels.

In Scripture, angels never appear as sweet little creatures who cuddle and coo. They're often described as God's army of mighty, fearless warriors wielding swords. In the King James Version of the Bible, an army is often called a "host" (see Exodus 15:4). God's angelic army is referred to many times as "the Lord's host," or the "host of heaven" (see 1 Kings 22:19), which leads us to another fallacy about angels.

Warrior or Wimp?

The fantasy: Angels are sweet, harmless creatures. **The biblical fact:** Angels are most often portrayed as warriors bearing swords.

Joshua, successor to Moses and leader of the Israelites into the Promised Land, was a mighty warrior himself. The Bible describes one night as Joshua was out walking alone on the eve of the Israelite army's battle against Jericho. Suddenly, he came upon a "man with a sword drawn in his hand" (Joshua 5:13). Joshua didn't immediately recognize him as an angel, so he posed the question to this stranger, "Are you for us or for our adversaries?" In other words, "Whose side are you on?" The angel-warrior wisely replied, "Neither."

Here we have another reminder in the angel's blunt answer that angelic beings are altogether unlike human beings. They're creatures from another world and don't have an interest in taking sides in human scenarios. They serve only one high commander, God Almighty. The angel went on to say to Joshua, "But as Captain of the Lord's host, I have now come." Then Joshua fell on his face because he realized he had not encountered a friend or foe; he was face to face with an angel of God (v. 14).

The first mention of angels in the Bible is in a military context (Genesis 3). God placed the cherubim (remember, the winged category of angel), each with a flaming sword, at the entrance of the Garden of Eden to prevent Adam and Eve from returning once they had sinned. It was the first known occasion of angelic guard duty.

Throughout the Word of God, we see military references used for angels. When Jesus talked about them, He confirmed that they were at His immediate disposal. On the night before He was crucified, Roman soldiers arrested Him in the Garden of Gethsemane.

Peter, one of the disciples, tried to defend Jesus by drawing his sword. But Jesus rebuked him saying, "Put your sword back in its place, for all who draw the sword will die by the sword. Do you think I cannot call on my Father, and he will at once put at my disposal more than twelve legions of angels?" (Matthew 26:52–53).

A legion is a word for a military division of 6,000 soldiers. Isaiah 37:36 says that in one night, a single angel killed 185,000 enemy soldiers. Think of it—a single angel is strong enough to defeat an entire army. Imagine what a legion of angels can do.

I am in awe at the power and impact of Jesus' statement. Throughout the entire ordeal of His trial, torture and crucifixion, He could have simply asked the Father and 72,000 angels would have been instantly dispatched for His aid. Try to imagine yourself as an angel during those moments in which God the Son was being brutally victimized by sinful man. It must have been agonizing for them to watch helplessly as man, the creature, abused God the Creator. I can imagine the angel army poised on the ramparts of heaven with swords drawn, listening for the Father to give the divine "go ahead" so these at-the-ready warriors could rescue their Lord.

Poised to Protect

A single mother once told me about the agonizing nights she spent in fear the first few weeks after her husband left her. The following account is an example of angels as warriors:

"My husband left me alone with two daughters. He left us many times, but this was final and I knew I'd have to adjust to raising my daughters by myself. I was always scared at night when I was alone. We lived on the outskirts of town, and every noise scared me. I could never sleep at night, so I paced the floor. I used to go to my baby's crib and rock her for hours during the night. One night, I returned home from my teaching job, exhausted from being up the night before. The thought of caring for my girls and then facing another night alone was almost overwhelming.

"I don't know how long I'd been alone when I saw my angel. During the night, I was walking 'my path' around the house, going from room to room. I passed the patio door and barely peeked out the curtain. At the opposite corner of the concrete slab of the patio stood my guard, in armor with a sword. I remember closing the curtain real fast, and when I looked again he was gone. I went to check on the girls, and then I went to bed. I slept every night after that. I wasn't scared about nighttime anymore.

"I still see that guard in my mind, but I've never seen him physically again, as I did that night. Still, I have no doubts of what I saw and the peace I felt."[1]

How many angels are there? The Bible says only God knows the exact number. We don't know, but we believe there's a set number. In Revelation 5:11, John records, "Then I looked and heard the voice of many angels, numbering thousands upon thousands, and ten thousand times ten thousand." That's an overwhelming number of angels—one hundred million to be exact.

However, even this isn't a definitive number because it's a term often used to describe something "beyond number." Interestingly, only three angels are named in the New International Version (NIV) of the Bible—Michael, Gabriel and Lucifer, the fallen angel. All the angels have names, but the Bible doesn't specify the names of any except these three. "Michael" is the archangel and "Gabriel" is a special messenger angel. "Lucifer" is a fallen angel referred to as the devil.

What Do Angels Do in Their Spare Time?

The fantasy: Angels are primarily occupied singing and playing harps. **The biblical fact:** The Bible never says angels play harps, nor does it say they sing.

I was both surprised and skeptical when I first learned that fact while reading W.A. Criswell's commentary on Revelation.[2] For over fifty years, Dr. Criswell served as the esteemed pastor of First Baptist Church in Dallas. In his commentary, he mentioned that the Bible never says angels sing. I couldn't believe it. I actually took my Bible and began a search to disprove his claim.

After thoroughly researching all of Scripture, I never found one verse that mentions angels singing (nor strumming harps, by the way). We actually get most of our ideas about angels singing from Christmas carols and hymns, like *Angels We Have Heard on High,* in which one of the verses says, "Angels we have heard on high, Sweetly singing o'er the plains." It's a beautiful hymn, but the Bible never says angels sing.

Some have claimed that Job 38:7 refers to angels singing. In that passage, it mentions the "morning stars" singing at Creation. Some believe those "morning stars" are angels, and if they are, then the Bible *does* say angels sing. But most commentators say it's just one of the Bible's many literary devices that personify nature. For example, the Bible also says, "The trees of the field shall clap their hands" (Isaiah 55:12).

Of course, that doesn't mean the trees literally erupt into applause. It's merely a figure of speech that expresses God's praise. Another reason I don't think "morning stars" are angels is because the next line in Job 38:7 says, "...and all the angels shouted for joy." Angels shout praises, but we never read of them singing.

You may be thinking, "What about the account in Luke 2, when the shepherds were out in the field and Jesus was born? Even though we sing it in Christmas musicals, the Bible says they *spoke* the words, "Glory to God in the highest, and on earth peace to men on whom his favor rests." (Luke 2:13–14).

One of the first verbs conjugated by Bible students in Greek 101 is the Greek word *lego*, which means "to speak." That's the exact word used in Luke 2:13. Look it up for yourself—I once had to do the very same thing. "Suddenly a great company of the heavenly host appeared with the angel, praising God and *saying,* 'Glory to God in the highest...' " (Luke 2:13, emphasis added).

Now, I hope I haven't ruined your Christmas spirit! For certain, the Bible never specifically teaches that angels sing. However, if you want to believe they do, go right ahead. You may be right, and if you are, when we discover the truth in heaven, I'll certainly agree with you. For now, I agree with Dr. Criswell, who said he'd keep on thinking and speaking of angels singing and the celestial choir, despite the fact the Bible didn't confirm that idea.[3]

We Have a Reason to Sing

You may wonder what the significance of this point is. I believe that, according to the Scriptures, the only people who really have the right and responsibility to sing praise are God's saints, born-again Christians. Angels have never been lost nor saved. They don't know the joy of salvation as we do.

You say, "What about in Revelation? Doesn't it say the angels will gather around and sing to the Lamb on the throne?" Check it out. Again, it says the angels *speak* their praise, but the saints *sing* a new song (Revelation 5:9)!

Revelation 4:8 speaks of the angels continually chanting praise to the Lamb, who is Jesus, on the throne. The Greek word is *legontas* (from the word *lego*—to speak). However, Revelation 5:9 speaks of the twenty-four elders *singing* a new song. I believe these elders represent all the redeemed of the ages. That's what we'll be doing one day in heaven—singing praise to the Savior.

Later in the chapter, when the angels join the chorus, the word *legontas* (to speak) is used (see Revelation 5:12, 13.) Although some English Bibles translate it "singing," the original language means, "to speak."

Have you ever heard someone say, "I wish I could sing like an angel?" Perhaps angels are the ones saying, "I wish I could sing like a saint!" I suspect there are some bewildered angels in many of our worship services when they see sullen-faced worshipers. Surely, they must resist the urge to nudge the person who doesn't sing from his or her heart and say, "C'mon, sing!" What a privilege it is to sing praises to God.

What Eyes Can't See

The fantasy: Angels must be seen to be real. **The biblical fact:** Angels are usually invisible; God only enables us at times to see them.

As a pastor with a keen interest in angels, the first question many people ask me is, "Have you ever encountered an angel?" I always answer, "I believe I have." I've already shared one personal encounter in this book. And you'll read about some other angel stories I believe to be true as well. However, if you ask me whether I've ever physically seen an angel, I'd have to reply, "I'm not sure."

If you're a follower of Jesus, there's a good chance you've encountered angels as well, but you might not have recognized them. In Hebrews 13:2, a fascinating passage about angels says, "Do not forget to entertain strangers, for by so doing some people have entertained angels without knowing it."

The King James Version employs the phrase that some have "entertained angels unawares." Whether or not you've ever realized it, you may have encountered angels—and you may encounter many more in your lifetime. Nevertheless, I *would* like to see an angel, and you probably would, too. Actually, sometimes angels are probably more willing to be seen than we imagine.

I believe we don't actually see more angels because we'd be tempted to do what the apostle John did. In the Book of Revelation, we read that when he encountered a glorious angel on the island of Patmos during his lonely exile, he instinctively fell down to worship it. The angel strongly objected, saying, "Do not do it! I am a fellow servant with you and with your brothers the prophets and of all who keep the words of this book. Worship God!" (Revelation 22:9).

I suspect that if you saw one of God's holy angels, you'd be so transfixed by the vision that you too would want to fall on your face in worship. However, remember angels aren't meant to be worshipped (Colossians 2:18). While we study angels, we must constantly draw our devotion back to the Lord Jesus Christ and to God the Father, who has blessed us with these angels.

Those who are so obsessed with the presence of angels come dangerously close to worshipping them. While God primarily keeps angels hidden from our sight, they themselves don't care to be recognized, and become alarmed at the idea that people would worship them.

Limited Perception

Our human perception is not all that highly developed, even when compared to the perception of God's other creatures. For instance, most of us don't smell very well. (By that, I mean our olfactory sense isn't as highly developed as that of other animals.)

For example, if you were a dog in a room full of people, you'd be able to detect each person's individual odor. Thankfully, our perception isn't as sensitive as a dog's when it comes to smelling.

Neither is our sense of hearing as refined as that of other creatures. Some animals can hear ultrasound—so high-pitched it's beyond our auditory range. Again, a dog's ears can pick up the sound of a high-frequency "silent whistle." There are other animals that can hear infrasound—extremely low, sonic waves we can't detect. Elephants and whales hear these sounds that are too low for human hearing. Our hearing range is actually limited to only a narrow band.

The same is true of our sense of vision. Some of God's creatures can see much better than we can, even with our glasses. A hawk or an eagle can detect the movement of a rat in tall grass from a great altitude. Even a common house-fly with over a hundred eyes is able to detect things differently than we can. The fact that we can't see everything with our eyes isn't our fault. God intentionally created us with a limited sense of perception.

Chapter 6 of 2 Kings teaches us all a lesson we need to learn if we ever hope to see an angel. It's the story of the prophet Elisha and his servant who found themselves surrounded by the army of the Arameans. Across the valley was an entire army of Aramean soldiers arrayed against them.

The servant was frightened at the prospect of facing off against the Aramean troops alone. Trembling, he asked, "What are we going to do, master?"

Elisha replied, "Those that are with us are more than those who are with them" (2 Kings 6:16).

I can imagine the dumbfounded servant saying, "What? There are only two of us! And look at all of them—there must be hundreds and thousands of them. What are you talking about?"

Elisha prayed a powerful one-sentence prayer, "O Lord, open his eyes so he may see" (2 Kings 6:17).

The Bible says the servant's eyes were opened and that he suddenly saw the mountains full of flaming chariots, horses and soldiers. An army of angelic warriors was there to support them. They'd been there all along; the servant just couldn't see them. God simply granted Elisha's servant the supernatural ability to see what was already there.

God sometimes peels back the curtain of our limited human perception and allows us to see angels, too. I believe that if God would open our spiritual eyes, we'd be amazed at the angelic activity surrounding us.

In the Bible, God promises to send His angels to help you, to protect you, and sometimes to deliver messages, but the angels usually are helpers hidden from our view. Only rarely does He allow us to visually perceive them.

The following encounter by a missionary to Africa portrays this truth:

"There was an African man named Abali who was a carpenter. He wanted to start churches, so the Foreign Mission Board gave him a little motorcycle to use in his travels. Abali had the desire to minister to a church that was on the other side of a steep, desolate mountain.

"On that mountain there was a rugged trail that followed a ledge around the mountain. The trail practically went straight up and down. As he was riding his motorcycle, he came to a place where the ledge had fallen and there was a makeshift bridge made of two logs and some boards.

"Abali climbed off his motorcycle and cautiously pushed it across the precarious bridge. Just as he was reaching the other side, the boards beneath his feet collapsed and he fell through. He had his legs and one arm holding on to a log and the other arm holding the motorcycle to keep it from falling. Abali could not pull himself up without letting go of the motorcycle and losing his only means of transportation.

"He cried out, helplessly, 'God, Help me!'

"No sooner had the words left his mouth than an old African man appeared carrying a basket. He asked Abali in his native tribal tongue, 'What can I do to help you?'

"Abali told him to take the motorcycle and push it on across. The man walked around him, set his basket down and pushed the motorcycle across. Abali pulled himself up, carefully walked on across and looked up to thank the man, but he had disappeared.

"Abali got on his motorcycle, knowing he could overtake the man since he was on foot, but he never saw him again. As Abali thought about it, he realized that the man must have been an angel. For what would an old man have been doing on foot so far from any village? How would the man have known his unique tribal tongue? How would the man have known that Abali was even from that specific tribe? And how could he have disappeared so quickly? An angel is the only explanation."[4]

Not All Angels Are Good

Angels really do exist, but most people choose to embrace fantasies about them. Maybe you've never really appreciated their existence and accepted their help because you've yet to believe what the Bible says about them. As you open your mind to the truth about angels, God can more easily open your eyes to see the ministry of angels around you and the reality of what's referred to as "spiritual warfare."

You see, not all angels are good angels. In fact, of the three angels named in the Bible, one of them is Lucifer—a fallen angel who rebelled against God and is currently at war with Him. We must recognize that he and his other fallen angel cohorts are just as real as the ministering spirits, or good angels.

Who are the devil's angels? They're sometimes called demons or evil spirits. Just as angels are ministering spirits, the devil has his assistants who are malevolent spirits.

At one time, Lucifer was an angel who enjoyed a high-ranking position of honor as a cherub. However, he tried to rebel against God and was cast out of heaven. Now he's called Satan, the devil. Some commentators believe that when Lucifer rebelled against God, many angels chose to join him. Some interpret Revelation 12:4 to mean that one-third of the angels were swept from heaven with Lucifer.

Angels are similar to human beings in this one respect—they have a will, and they can exercise choice. Several of them deliberately chose to join Lucifer in the rebellion against God.

Some people often ask why a loving God ever created a hell. Jesus gives us the answer and at the same moment teaches us something about angels. In one of His teachings, He said, "Depart from me, you who are cursed, into the eternal fire prepared for the devil and his angels" (Matthew 25:41). Because He is loving and compassionate, God never desired for human beings to inhabit hell—it was specifically created and reserved for Satan and the fallen angels.

However, whenever a person rejects God's love and His free gift of eternal life, that individual is choosing his or her own hellish destiny for eternity. God does not "send" people to hell. People exercise their free will to choose God or reject Him.

Is Satan Real?

Among those who claim to believe in God, many don't claim to believe in a living being called the devil. In fact, this disparity is an interesting part of Satan's grand strategy. Satan doesn't necessarily want people to worship him; he doesn't want us to believe in him at all. Why not? He knows that if a person doesn't believe in him, he or she won't be on guard against his attacks.

That's why the apostle Peter warned, "Be self-controlled and alert. Your enemy the devil prowls around like a roaring lion looking for someone to devour. Resist him, standing firm in the faith, because you know that your brothers throughout the world are undergoing the same kind of sufferings" (1 Peter 5:8-9).

In his movie, *The Passion of the Christ*, Mel Gibson cast Satan as a frightening androgynous creature. If you met up with this wild-eyed character in the street, you'd be sure to avoid him at all costs. However, Satan doesn't necessarily want to frighten us; instead, he prefers to entice us.

If our picture of Satan is a repulsive, scary creature, we must think again. He's like some of the participants on the television show, "Extreme Makeover," who are almost unrecognizable due to the changes to their appearance afforded by plastic surgery. Satan can appear as someone or something beautiful and attractive and not at all like something we would naturally fear. The Bible says in 2 Corinthians 11:15: "Satan himself masquerades *as an angel of light*" (emphasis added).

We can't necessarily recognize Satan by the way he looks, but we can recognize his voice. He is a liar. Jesus said, "...The devil...was a murderer from the beginning, not holding to the truth, for there is no truth in him. When he lies, he speaks his native language, for he is a liar and the father of lies" (John 8:44).

I believe Satan has succeeded in convincing most Americans to believe his three greatest lies: 1) that he doesn't really exist; 2) that evil is good and good is evil; and 3) that we can sin and we will not suffer. In order to understand how Satan and his demons work against us, we need to recognize him as real, develop a biblical respect for him and consistently resist him.

---

[1] As told by Karen Hawthorn.

[2] Criswell, W.A., Expository Sermons on Revelation, vol. 3 (Grand Rapids, MI: Zondervan Publishing House), 82-83.

[3] Ibid, 82-83

[4] As told by Doug Knapp, International Mission Board missionary to Tanzania.

CHAPTER 4

The Terrible Toothless Lion

In the winter of 2004, California cyclist Anne Hjelle miraculously survived being mauled by a mountain lion. The 30-year-old was cycling with a friend in a popular wilderness park in Southern California when the animal attacked her from behind. The women were completely unaware that earlier that same afternoon a male cyclist had actually been killed by a mountain lion in that very spot. His ravaged body was later discovered hidden in the underbrush.

As the giant cat seized Anne by the neck and tried to drag her into the bushes, her friend and several other riders threw rocks at the animal to prod it to release her. Witnesses said the animal clenched her entire head in its jaws, likely attempting to break her neck. Desperate, her fellow cyclist grabbed her leg and engaged in a violent tug of war with the lion until it gave up and ran off. In several television and newspaper interviews following her slow and painful recovery, Anne credited her faith in God for her miraculous survival.

Like the mountain lion in this tragic story, our spiritual enemy, the devil, relentlessly prowls around looking for an easy target. Many before us have crossed his path and suffered a terrible fate, and yet he's not satisfied. The Bible says, "Be self-controlled and alert. Your enemy the devil prowls around like a roaring lion looking for someone to devour. Resist him, standing firm in the faith, because you know that your brothers throughout the world are undergoing the same kind of sufferings," 1 Peter 5:8–9.

Much like its cousin, the mountain lion, an African lion is one of the most formidable and powerful animals in God's creation. The "king of the beasts" can grow to more than eight feet in length (not counting his tail) and weigh over 400 pounds. He can snap a zebra's neck with a single bite or crush the skull of a warthog with one swipe of his mighty paw. Studying the hunting methods of African lions, I've found several similarities between Satan and lions that will help us appreciate the biblical imagery of a lion on the prowl.

A Sneaky Strategy

The preferred hunting method of lions is to hide themselves near a water hole or trail and wait for an unsuspecting animal to pass by. Then, with a roar that paralyzes their prey with fear, they spring out of hiding and it's lunch time.

Lions are naturally equipped with a camouflage color that matches the African plains, and they're patient enough to wait for hours. Like a lion, the devil is sneaky in his strategy. He always hides his true intent. He never tries to get an individual to hate God; he just wants him or her to doubt the truth about God. Wherever God puts a period, the devil puts a question mark.

In the Garden of Eden, the first recorded words of the devil are a question. He asked Eve, "Did God really say 'you must not eat from any tree in the Garden?'" (Genesis 3:1). That's not what God had said at all (see Genesis 2:15–17), but Satan twisted God's word in his question. He's still using the covert approach today.

Satan would never specifically say to someone, "Don't believe God." That's too direct. Instead, he'll plant seeds of doubt. "Is the Bible really the Word of God?" "Is Jesus really the only way to heaven?" "Is there really a heaven and a hell?" His strategy begins with subtle doubts, not necessarily a full-out attack. Like a hungry lion sizing up a herd of gazelles on the plain, looking for any sign of weakness, he's cunning and he's patient.

Stalking His Prey

Unlike cheetahs who can reach speeds up to 70 mph, lions aren't the fastest animal in the jungle. Therefore, they've become experts at silently slipping up on their unsuspecting prey. When they get close enough to their target, they spring forward with a quick burst of speed.

The first chapter of Job gives us a behind-the-scenes look at how Satan similarly stalks his prey. The chapter opens with the first of two discussions God and Satan had about a righteous man named Job. Satan comes before God and God asks him what he had been doing. God, of course, already knew the answer to the question. But pay attention to Satan's reply.

Satan says he has just returned "from roaming through the earth and going back and forth in it" (Job 1:7). In other words, he was on the prowl, looking for someone to attack, and he had already targeted Job as his next victim. Despite our culture's comic interpretations, Satan is not a character with horns, dressed in red flannel underwear and mindlessly shoveling coal down in hell.

In fact, this passage in Job is a sober reminder that Satan isn't in hell. He's roaming throughout the earth, stalking his prey.

If you're familiar with this fascinating story, you know Satan had been watching Job. He saw that he was a righteous man who loved God with all his heart. He also saw that God had blessed him. So, Satan set out to prove that Job's faith would falter if God permitted Satan to test him and destroy his blessings—several thousand grazing animals and his family.

This celestial conversation emphasizes again the number of activities constantly taking place all around us in the spiritual dimension. Job could hear his donkeys braying and his sheep bleating, but he couldn't hear the conversation going on between God and Satan. Oblivious, all Job could see was that some really terrible stuff suddenly began to happen in his life—he lost his herds, many of his servants, and he even lost his children to some catastrophic events.

Job could easily see what was happening all around him in the physical, earthly realm. However, he couldn't see what had transpired in the spiritual realm, so he didn't understand why he was undergoing these trials. Today, when we read Job's story, we have the benefit of hindsight, but Job didn't.

Whenever you want to pull out your hair and ask, "What in the world is going on?" Remember, it's not "what in *this* world is going on." It's what's in *that* world that's really going on!

Satan Opposes You

Not only does Job's story illustrate Satan stalking his prey, it reminds us how much he desires to attack the saints. Satan opposes every potential servant of God. The name "Satan" literally means "adversary." Satan does not maintain a neutral approach to humans; he wants to make your life miserable. That's why Satan said to God about Job, "Stretch out your hand and strike everything he has, and he will surely curse you to your face" (Job 1:11). Satan is actively, aggressively and continually working to try to make people curse God to His face.

He hates you personally, so insert your name into the blank: Satan *"prowls around like a roaring lion looking for (your name) to devour."* We shouldn't admire the devil, but we must respect his power. Circus lion tamers who lose respect for the lions in their cage may end up losing an arm—or worse. According to John 10:10, Satan's strategy for your life is to "steal and kill and destroy." He wants to steal your blessings, kill your joy and destroy your happiness.

The Sinister Minister of Fear

Zoologists say a lion's roar is the loudest noise made by a living creature. On a still night in the open plains of Africa, it can be heard almost five miles away. The roar has been recorded at close to 100 decibels at a distance of 200 yards—that's comparable with the volume of a rock concert.

While there's no clear consensus on why a lion roars, many scientists believe it does so to terrorize its prey. In some cases, the lion paralyzes his prey with fear for a crucial short second—all the time it needs to pounce.

In the same way, Satan's most effective methods are his scare tactics. Worldwide terrorism has people cringing in fear. We live in a time when terror alerts and biological threats are part of our modern vernacular. However, the Bible says God does not want us to live in bondage to the sinister minister of fear, the devil. "For God did not give us a spirit of timidity, but a spirit of power, of love and of self-discipline" (2 Timothy 1:7). If Satan can keep us paralyzed with fear, he can defeat us.

However, there *is* good news. The Bible tells us in 1 Peter 5:9 that we must resist the devil, *"standing firm in the faith."* Sure, Satan appears to be a powerful, frightening beast, but have you realized he's actually an old toothless lion? Once you make that discovery in God's Word, you don't have to live in fear anymore.

A Toothless Lion

Of all Aesop's fables, one of the strangest and most obscure is entitled, "The Lion in Love." Consisting of only five sentences, it's also one of the shortest fables.

> A Lion demanded the daughter of a Woodcutter in marriage. The Father, unwilling to grant, and yet afraid to refuse his request, came up with this plan to deal with the Lion. He expressed his willingness to accept the Lion as the suitor of his daughter on one condition: that the Lion should allow him to extract his teeth, and cut off his claws, as his daughter was fearfully afraid of both. The Lion cheerfully assented to the proposal. But when the toothless, clawless Lion returned to request to marry his daughter, the Woodcutter, no longer afraid, set upon him with his club, and drove him away into the forest.

According to the Bible, that's what Jesus has done to the old toothless lion, Satan. He has ultimately rendered him powerless. He's a defeated foe. Like the lion in this fable, the Bible describes the devil skulking away with his tail between his legs whenever we resist him in Jesus' name. "Submit yourselves, then, to God. Resist the devil, and he will flee from you" (James 4:7).[1]

The Lion of Judah

Resisting the devil is a basic tenet of spiritual warfare—a subject that often arises in any discussion on spiritual beings, angels and demons. The best way to resist the devil is to understand and claim the victory Jesus has already won. The devil really has no power over us, because of what Jesus did on the cross. The Bible says in 1 John 3:8, "The reason the Son of God appeared was to destroy the devil's work."

Elsewhere, the Bible says, "The lions may roar and growl, yet the teeth of the great [old] lions are broken" (Job 4:10, parentheses added). On the cross, Jesus broke the teeth of that roaring lion, Satan.

When a male lion roars in the jungle, all the animals tremble with fear *except one:* another bigger, stronger male lion. In fact, this lion heads *toward* the sound of the roar to challenge that lion for supremacy in the wild. Did you know the Bible says there's another lion far superior to the roaring lion, Satan? Revelation 5:5 says, "Do not weep! See, the Lion of the tribe of Judah, the Root of David, has triumphed!" On the cross, Jesus Christ triumphed over Satan.

Angels Could Have Saved Jesus

The cross was the only way to fulfill God's plan to save humanity from sin and defeat Satan once and for all. Remember how, on the night of Jesus' arrest, legions of warrior angels were poised at the ramparts of heaven to save Him? We know He could have called for them, but why didn't He? Look at what he said to Simon Peter that night: "But how then would the Scriptures be fulfilled that say it must happen in this way?" (Matthew 26:54). Jesus was so conscious of fulfilling God's Word that He refused to call for angelic help. Jesus demonstrated such stubborn love for us that He suffered silently when help was only a prayer away.

At the beginning of creation, God described the moment of victory when Jesus would be crucified and resurrected from the dead. "And I will put enmity between you and the woman, and between your offspring and hers; he will crush your head, and you will strike his heel" (Genesis 3:15). He promised that one day the seed of woman (Jesus) would crush the head of the serpent (Satan).

What does this mean? At the cross, the serpent "struck the heel" of Jesus, but it wasn't a fatal blow. Jesus "crushed the serpent's head" by coming back from the dead, victorious over sin and death, sealing Satan's fate that will be revealed at the end of time. "The devil, who deceived them, was thrown into the lake of burning sulphur, [to be] tormented day and night forever and ever" (Revelation 20:10).

This Means War

The Bible makes it clear that spiritual warfare is a reality. Satan knows his time on earth is limited and he is out to destroy as much of God's creation as possible. History is replete with horrible atrocities that serve as reminders of the fact that there is a devil, bent on the destruction of the human race. Our only hope is God's promise that says, "Greater is he that is in you, than he that is in the world" (1 John 4:4, KJV).

Although I'm not one to exaggerate the existence of demons (the devil doesn't deserve that much of our attention), I'm convinced there's an invisible world of spiritual conflict raging around us. The Bible instructs us to take it seriously.

> So take everything the Master has set out for you, well-made weapons of the best materials. And put them to use so you will be able to stand up to everything the Devil throws your way. This is no afternoon athletic contest that we'll walk away from and forget about in a couple of hours. This is for keeps, a life-or-death fight to the finish against the Devil and all his angels. (Ephesians 6:11–12, The Message)

The spiritual struggle we see throughout the Bible is real. It continues to this day. Satan and his organized legions of angels are constantly working to thwart God's plans.

However, because it is an invisible battle, we wield our weapons primarily in prayer. "The weapons we fight with are not the weapons of the world. On the contrary, they have divine power to demolish strongholds. We demolish arguments and every pretension that sets itself up against the knowledge of God, and we take captive every thought to make it obedient to Christ" (2 Corinthians 10:4–5).

Rules of Engagement

In a war, there are certain rules of engagement that define how battle takes place, including the limitations, directives, etc. The dictionary defines it this way:

> **rules of engagement:** *n. pl.* A directive issued by competent military authority that delineates the limitations and circumstances under which forces will initiate and prosecute combat engagement with other forces encountered.[2]

When we consider spiritual warfare, there are certain rules of engagement that define the battle that's taking place around us every day. We can summarize these rules of engagement in three words we use in exclusive reference to God that should never be used to describe angels, Satan or his demons.

First, God is *omnipresent.* That means the presence of God permeates every part of the universe. Angels are not omnipresent; they cannot be everywhere at once. Remember, Satan is only a fallen angel himself. Therefore, he is not omnipresent. Unlike God, Satan cannot be everywhere at once. However, he has an organized, demonized army of fallen angels to assist him in his devilish strategy. Assuming Satan can be everywhere at once is a dangerous belief because it ascribes to a fallen angel an attribute that belongs only to the living God.

Second, God is *omniscient.* That means God knows everything. We're mistaken if we think angels know everything. Again, even Satan, the fallen angel, doesn't know everything. He's smarter than most of us; he's certainly clever and subtle, but don't ever say he's omniscient. Satan only knows what God allows him to know.

Third, God is *omnipotent.* That means God alone is all-powerful. Angels are powerful, but only God is all-powerful. Likewise, Satan is not all-powerful.

Spiritual Peripheral Vision

Although this book mainly emphasizes the truth about angels, while providing a wider understanding of demonic activity and spiritual warfare, our focus should always be on the Lord Jesus Christ.

Many people are interested in the topic of angels and demons because they're fascinated with the supernatural. You've already read several accounts in this book from individuals who believe they've encountered angels. As remarkable as an experience with an angel and/or spiritual warfare is, we must remember to keep our eyes firmly focused on the Lord Jesus Christ, who has provided us with these angelic helpers.

When we think about angels, I recommend we use our spiritual peripheral vision. Sometimes, when we look directly at a star at night, we cannot see it; but when we look to the side, our eyes are able to focus on a clearer picture of that star. When it comes to angels, our focus should be squarely on Jesus.

We should imitate the author of Hebrews and fix our eyes on Jesus, the "author and perfecter of our faith" (Hebrews 12:2). Using our spiritual peripheral vision, we can keep Jesus centrally in view and be aware of the presence of God's ministering spirits.

A Mighty Fortress Is Our God

Almost five hundred years ago, Martin Luther penned that wonderful hymn, *A Mighty Fortress Is Our God*, to remind us there's great spiritual warfare occurring around us. When we sing it, we often miss the point of the message. In the first two verses, Martin Luther wrote about God's greatness, then he began to talk about the devil.

For still our ancient foe
Doth seek to work us woe;
His craft and pow'r are great,
And armed with cruel hate,
On earth is not his equal.

Luther is correct. Satan is powerful, and no person on earth can match his diabolical power. However, God is infinitely more powerful, as expressed in the climax of this beautiful hymn.

That word above all earthly pow'rs,
No thanks to them, abideth;
The Spirit and the gifts are ours
Thro' him who with us sideth.
Let goods and kindred go,
This mortal life also;
The body they may kill;
God's truth abideth still:
His kingdom is forever.
-Martin Luther (1483 – 1546)

---

[1] Victoria Boyson has written a great article entitled, "It Will Be Worth It!" that speaks about Satan's defeat. Her website, www.boyson.org, is worth consulting.

[2] *The American Heritage Dictionary of the English Language*, Fourth Edition, Houghton Mifflin Company, 2000.

CHAPTER FIVE

Who's Who Among Angels

He didn't speak English and we didn't speak Russian. He just kept nodding and pointing to the sky. We tried to ask him the name of the mysterious man's face on the dial of his watch. But he just met our questions with a smile and a nod toward the sky. We wrinkled our brows and wondered, "Is he meaning Jesus or God?"

When a missionary group from our church was in the former Soviet Union one summer, we bought some watches from a street vendor. On the band was a figure of a man's face. We tried to ask the vendor who that person was, but we didn't have a translator.

We finally discovered that it was a picture of the first Soviet cosmonaut, Yuri Gagarin, a hero to the Soviet people. In 1961, Gagarin made history as the first man to go into space. He came back to earth and made his famous statement, "I've been to the heavens and I did not see God." Ten years later, Yuri Gagarin died mysteriously in a plane crash. (By the way, that *is* when he saw God.)

It's interesting that years later, some of the Soviet cosmonauts gave a very different report about heaven or space. A nationally syndicated newspaper printed an article about six Soviet cosmonauts who witnessed the most awe-inspiring spectacle ever encountered in space—a band of glowing angels as big as jumbo jets.

What they saw, the space travelers said, were seven giant figures in forms of humans with mist-like halos, as in the classic depiction of angels. Their faces were round with cherubic smiles. Twelve days later, the figures returned and were seen by three other Soviet scientists, including female cosmonaut Elana Stepharich. "They were smiling," she said, "as though they shared in a glorious secret."[1] It's no secret that the angels have a lot to smile about—after all, they're in constant contact with the loving God of the universe, praising him and doing his bidding.

As their Supreme Commander, God has organized the heavenly host into an army of many divisions and ranks. God is not a God of confusion, but exact order. Those who have served in the military understand the importance of organization and rank—the difference between a private, sergeant, lieutenant, captain and major, up to general and commander in chief.

In God's army, there is also order and division. For example, remember Joshua's encounter with an angel in a shining garment as he was preparing to attack Jericho? The angel identified himself as "commander of the host of the Lord" (Joshua 5:14, KJV). The word *host* is used to describe a powerful army. This angel was a captain in God's angelic army, one of many roles assigned among the angels.

Let's take a look at the various divisions of angels and see who's who among the angel ranks.

Archangel

The Bible describes the archangel Michael (Jude 9), who is one of the three angels named in the Bible. We often think there are several archangels, but the Bible identifies only Michael as the archangel. We can consider the archangel as a type of prime minister, commander or chief. In his seventeen-volume epic, *Paradise Lost,* John Milton incorrectly identifies Gabriel as one of the archangels. The Bible never gives this title to Gabriel.

The Bible also teaches that when Jesus returns, Michael will be the one to announce it with a shout (1 Thessalonians 4:16). This verse says there will be the sound of the trumpet as well. Popular music has also erroneously identified Gabriel as the angel who'll blow the horn. While this belief may be popular in the French Quarter of New Orleans, it's foreign to the Bible. We have no idea who'll play the trumpet when Jesus returns to earth.

Although we seldom see Michael in the Bible, Jude 9 tells us about a particular dispute between Satan and Michael. "But even the archangel Michael, when he was disputing with the devil about the body of Moses, did not dare to bring a slanderous accusation against him, but said, 'The Lord rebuke you!'"

Moses, who led the Israelites out of bondage in Egypt, died at the age of 120. The Bible describes a special relationship between God and His servant, Moses. "The Lord would speak to Moses face to face, as a man speaks with his friend..." (Exodus 33:11). In fact, at his death, Deuteronomy 34:6 says God buried him in a valley near Moab and no one else knew where his grave lay. In His perfect plan, God wanted to bring Moses' body to heaven so he, along with the prophet Elijah, would be able to stand on the Mount of Transfiguration with Jesus (see Matthew 17:1–13). Apparently the devil, who delights in death and the grave, did not agree to this plan.

The word "dispute" means "to fight." Michael and the devil fought over his body. However, it's comforting to see that the devil was no match for Michael, the archangel, because Moses did indeed appear with Jesus on the Mount of Transfiguration.

Seraphim

The Bible speaks of another division of angels besides the archangel. These are the seraphim. In Hebrew, when the suffix "im" is added, it makes that word plural. One of these angels would be called a *seraph*, and more than one would be called *seraphim.*

The Old Testament prophetic book, Isaiah, introduces us to these angelic creatures. Isaiah sees a vision of the greatness of God and part of his vision includes the seraphim. He describes them in the following way:

> In the year that King Uzziah died, I saw the Lord seated on a throne, high and exalted, and the train of his robe filled the temple. Above him were seraphs, each with six wings: With two wings they covered their faces, with two they covered their feet, and with two they were flying. And they were calling to one another: "Holy, holy, holy is the Lord Almighty; the whole earth is full of his glory."
> (Isaiah 6:1–3)

Remember, we've already established that the Bible seldom describes what we've termed *God's holy angels* as possessing wings. However, we also concluded that this unique category of angels does, based on biblical descriptions. In fact, in Revelation 4:6–8, the Apostle John sees four heavenly creatures, each with six wings praising God.

God created seraphim with the express purpose of praising and worshiping Him. Their job is to surround the throne of God and to render continual praise to Him. John wrote, "Day and night they never stop saying: Holy, Holy, Lord God Almighty, who was, and is, and is to come" (Revelation 4:8). Many scholars consider these the same heavenly beings described in Isaiah 6.

In John Bunyan's classic book, *Pilgrim's Progress*, the main character (Christian) sets out to find the Celestial City, heaven. Along the way, he meets a variety of characters, one of which is named Pliable. Pliable is curious about what Christian expects to find inside heaven's gates at the end of his journey. After hearing Christian describe a vision of eternal bliss and glory, Pliable asks, "And what company shall we have there?" In answer, Christian says, "There we shall be with Seraphims and Cherubims, Creatures that will dazzle your eyes to look on them."[2] Such is the beauty of these marvelous creatures we will one day see in heaven.

Cherubim

Beside the archangel and the seraphim, the Bible also speaks of cherubim. As with seraphim, *cherub* would be singular, with *cherubim* being plural. Scripture mentions cherubim many more times than seraphim, beginning with the angels posting guard outside the Garden of Eden in Genesis 3.

When God gave Moses the details for the construction of the tabernacle, He left instructions to place beautiful replicas of cherubim on top of the Ark of the Covenant. The mercy seat, placed on the top of the ark, was designed so that the two cherubim faced each other with their huge wings outstretched (2 Chronicles 5:8). Master weavers inlaid delicate figures of cherubim into the blue, purple and scarlet yarn that formed the curtain inside the tabernacle (Exodus 36:8) and Solomon instructed skilled craftsmen to do the same later inside the temple (2 Chronicles 3:14).

Angelic Flying Objects?

The prophet Ezekiel refers to cherubim nineteen times in his prophetic book. According to Ezekiel, cherubim have four wings as opposed to seraphim, who possess six (10:21). The tenth chapter of Ezekiel is an amazing description of these cherubim.

Ezekiel describes a fantastic vision of a dazzling wheel within a wheel, with the inner wheel turning one way and the outer wheel turning another way, rising and falling with the movement of the cherubim. When the cherubim rose, the wheels rose When the cherubim spread their wings, the entire vision itself, adorned with a bright array of lights, began to fly, with the ability to move suddenly in every direction.

In his book, *Angels: God's Secret Agents,* Billy Graham refers to the fact that many people believe that what some individuals have seen and considered to be UFOs through the years may literally be a vision of these cherubim.[3] The description of the color and size of many UFO accounts is amazingly similar to the description in Ezekiel 10.

You may be thinking, "Are you saying all UFOs are angels?" No, not at all. I'm just pointing out that many people, including some of the most respectable biblical scholars, have recognized the similarities with Ezekiel 10. Perhaps some of these UFOs actually could be AFOs—Angelic Flying Objects!

Ordinary Angels

While we don't know a great deal about Michael, the archangel, or seraphim and cherubim, the Bible is full of references to ordinary angels. Although we refer to this group as God's holy angels or common angels, there's nothing common about them. Gabriel would be considered one of these ordinary angels. His name means "God's hero."

We always see Gabriel in Scripture as a messenger angel—four times to be exact. On two occasions, Gabriel appears to the Old Testament character, Daniel, and ministers to him in his time of need.

In the New Testament, Gabriel appears to Zacharias, the soon-to-be father of John the Baptist, and also to Mary, the mother of Jesus. As further evidence that angels can often appear as ordinary men, there's no indication that this incredible vision of the angel Gabriel or the stunning announcement that Elizabeth was pregnant overwhelmed Zacharias (Luke 1:5–25). In fact, his first instinct was to disagree with Gabriel's message—as if arguing with a stranger on the street.

When Gabriel predicts that he'll become a father, Zacharias scoffs at the idea—after all, he believes he and his wife are too old. In response, Gabriel exercises his God-given power to take away Zacharias' voice for the next nine months because he didn't immediately believe God's message.

Gabriel is best-known for his appearance to a virgin named Mary, when he predicts that she'll give birth to God's Son, the Messiah (Luke 1:26–56). The Bible says God sent Gabriel to the town of Nazareth—where Mary was engaged to be married to a man named Joseph—with the good news. Angels touched Jesus' life from this moment throughout the duration of His time on earth.

There are many other biblical references to the appearance and activity of God's ordinary holy angels. You might be surprised at what you learn in the next chapter about the awesome strength and destructive power of God's angels. From the battlefields in ancient Israel to the cockpits of World War II airplanes, there is much to learn from these stories about angels in action.

---

1 USA Today, December 1990.

2 John Bunyah, Pilgrim's Progress, public domain.

3 Billy Graham, Angels: God's Secret Agents (Garden City, NY: Doubleday and Company, Inc., 1975) 15-16. I first became fascinated with angels many years ago when I read this book. In my opinion, it is still the finest book ever written on angels.

CHAPTER SIX

What Do Angels Do?

Many people envision heaven as a place where angels just sort of float around on clouds, singing hymns and strumming harps all day. While we're tempted to envision angels as sweet, docile beings, we've already shown how that portrayal comes from popular culture, not the Bible. The Bible describes angels as mighty warriors of God, poised at the ramparts of heaven to do His bidding.

When we recognize that angels comprise a great army for God, we begin to see many references in the Bible to their destructive strength. Angels often bring God's judgment upon a sinful nation, something their meek and mild depictions on the front of Christmas cards often misrepresent.

While part of the holy angels' job description is to carry out God's wrath in specific scenarios, we also find many stories in the Bible of angels bringing good news and helping deliver God's people. We read in Psalm 103:20, "Praise the Lord, you his angels, you mighty ones who do his bidding, who obey his word."

Angels excel in strength to obey whatever God tells them to do. They're always listening for a directive from their Commander in Chief, Jesus Christ. Let's look at some examples of the destructive power of God's angelic army.

Angels Visit Sodom

In Genesis 19, two angels came to the city of Sodom. This was a highly immoral city, because of the widespread practice of homosexuality. The angels came to visit Lot, the cousin of Abraham. The city had become so vile that the men of the city wanted to engage in sexual relations with these newcomers in town, little realizing they were angels.

The angels' message to Lot reveals their amazing strength to take down an entire city. "We are going to destroy this place. The outcry to the Lord against its people is so great that he has sent us to destroy it" (Genesis 19:13). Incredibly, two lone angels were equipped to render everything in sight to a pile of smoldering rubble.

God gave Abraham an opportunity for Sodom to be spared if he could find righteous people living there, but when Abraham was unable to find even ten righteous people, God's judgment was inevitable. God is a loving God, full of mercy and kindness, and He always gives people opportunity to repent. However, Sodom refused to repent, so the angelic agents of God's destruction brought the city to a fiery end.

Angel of Death

In Exodus 12, we read of another example of the destructive power of God's angels. When Pharaoh refused to allow the children of Israel to leave Egypt, God sent a series of plagues upon the land (Exodus 7–11). The Bible says Pharaoh's heart was hardened, and he stubbornly continued to resist Moses' pleas. So God unleashed a final deadly plague.

In preparation for the disastrous plague, God gave Moses specific instructions. Every Hebrew family should sacrifice a lamb without defect, sprinkle the blood on the doorframe, enter into the house for the night and eat the meat from the lamb. Any families not following these instructions would suffer the death of their firstborn—both children and animals (12:12).

However, included in the warning was the promise that every house duly covered with the blood of the sacrifice would be spared. Once again, we see a loving God offering a way to escape judgment.

That night, an angel visited the nation as God promised. In 1 Corinthians 10:10, this angel is called "the destroying angel," because he would carry out God's order to kill the firstborn.

You may have heard about the "Angel of Death" in literature and other extra-biblical sources—a spirit being who accompanies a person at the time of death. In a later chapter, we'll study what the Bible says about death, and who we can expect to escort us to heaven.

Under the darkness of night, this "destroyer" (Exodus 12:23) moved throughout the nation of Egypt, "passing over" the Hebrew homes protected by the blood of the lamb sprinkled on the doorposts. This is the origin of the Jewish celebration, Passover—a traditional meal commemorating Israel's deliverance from Egypt.

The absence of blood on the doorposts of a house was a sign to the destroying angel to release the plague of death on that household. Many thousands of Egyptians died because they refused to obey God's clear warning to release the Israelites from bondage.

In this story about the angel, we see an Old Testament picture of how Christ's blood saves us in a similar manner. The Bible says the penalty of sin is death (Romans 6:23)—not just physical death, but spiritual death—meaning eternal separation from God.

Like the sacrificial lamb at Passover, Jesus was the perfect, innocent sacrifice God required. No one else would do, because no one else in history lived a perfect, sinless life. When Jesus willingly shed His blood on the cross, He provided a way for God's wrath to "pass over" us and save us from certain death. The story of the angel at Passover has pointed to the cross of Jesus and salvation for generations.

Order Withdrawn

In 2 Samuel 24, we read about an unusual occurrence demonstrating the might of God's army of angels. God became angry at the nation of Israel because of their continual rebellion and idolatry. As a result, He sent an angel to deliver His judgment. Seventy thousand people were destroyed by a single mighty angel over a period of three days (2 Samuel 24:15–16).

In fact, the angel was ready with further orders to destroy the entire population. However, the Bible says the sight of the angel ready to carry out His command to destroy them touched God's heart and he ordered the angel to halt. At the same time, God allowed King David a preview of what was to come, as he saw the angel ominously poised over the city of Jerusalem.

In 1 Chronicles 21:16, the Bible describes this angel "standing between heaven and earth," extending a glistening sword over the city. After witnessing three days of horrific suffering, David developed a healthy fear regarding the awesome power at the angel's disposal. He didn't want the angel to exact any more of God's judgment. He prayed earnestly for God to withhold punishment—so much so that he was willing to take responsibility for the sins of the nation.

He said to God, "I am the one who has sinned and done wrong. These are but sheep. What have they done? Let your hand fall upon me and my family" (2 Samuel 24:17). In a spirit of humility and meekness, he asked God to punish him, but to spare the nation.

This is one of the most touching examples in the Bible of intercessory prayer. As a result, God decided to withdraw the angel's orders and not destroy the entire population of Jerusalem.

Single-Handed Syrian Massacre

There's also an exciting story in 2 Kings 19 about angelic assistance in a surprising victory of the army of Israel, when the Assyrians utterly surrounded and outnumbered them. The massive Assyrian army, more than 185,000 soldiers strong, lay siege to Israel. The outcome seemed hopeless and the Israelites cried out to God. However, during the night, a single warrior-angel boldly crossed into enemy territory to face the Assyrian army.

The Bible describes it this way, "That night the angel of the Lord went out and put to death a hundred and eighty-five thousand men in the Assyrian camp. When the people got up the next morning—there were all the dead bodies! So Sennacherib king of Assyria broke camp and withdrew. He returned to Nineveh and stayed there" (2 Kings 19:35–36).

Perhaps you're beginning to realize the strength and might represented in one single angel. Imagine the absolute power and might of God's angelic *army*!

The Death of Herod Agrippa

An egotistical maniac, Agrippa considered himself to be a king, although he was only a middle management governmental official. He relished the opportunity to sit on a throne, soaking in the worship and adoration of even the most fickle population. He temporarily gained favor with Christians by allowing the growth of what he interpreted to be a new sect of Judaism.

Then, when the surge in the number of Christians began to alarm the Jewish authorities, he allowed persecution to resume. Agrippa even arranged for the murder of the apostle, James, and put Peter in prison to await execution. However, Agrippa's time in the spotlight was short-lived.

In Acts 12:22–23, we read how Agrippa entertained the praises of a crowd after one of his speeches, even permitting them to acclaim him as a god. "Immediately, because Herod did not give praise to God, an angel of the Lord struck him down, and he was eaten by worms and died." That should serve as a stern warning to all of us to guard against arrogance! However, it can also be interpreted as a judgment against Agrippa for persecuting Christians.

These are just a few examples of the magnificent, destructive power of angels. Do these stories make it sound as though angels are sweet little creatures flitting about in heaven? When we someday meet the angels in heaven, I believe we'll most likely recognize them as formidable warriors.

An Army of Deliverance

It's somewhat scary to think about the destructive power of angels, but the good news is that for God's children, they serve as an army of deliverance. Angels are on the frontlines of spiritual warfare and they're fighting on our behalf. They encourage us and enable us to be victorious. In a later chapter, we'll look more in depth at the ways God's ministering spirits help us, but for now let's look at a few biblical and personal illustrations.

For example, at the same moment the angels were coming to destroy Sodom, they were also there to deliver Lot and his family from the impending disaster. They announced that judgment was coming, and offered to lead them out of danger.

In Genesis 19:15–16, we read, "With the coming of dawn, the angels urged Lot saying, 'Hurry! Take your wife and your two daughters who are here, or you will be swept away when the city is punished.' When he hesitated, the men grasped his hand and the hands of his wife and of his two daughters and led them safely out of the city, for the Lord was merciful to them."

That's a good example of the ministry of deliverance angels perform. Many times angels rescue us from danger. And sometimes invisible spiritual warfare even affects earthly warfare.

Angels in a World at War

There are many accounts from World War II of such a connection. I believe Adolf Hitler was a man deeply influenced by Satan and his demons. His plot to kill the Jews and conquer the world was hatched in hell. He wasn't a highly intelligent man, but there seemed to be an invisible force promoting him to his place of prominence.

During the war, our soldiers often carried small Bibles in their shirt pockets into battle. I recall one veteran showing me his Bible. A German bullet had punctured it, traveling halfway through until it stopped in Psalm 91. What does Psalm 91:11 say? "For he will command his angels concerning you to guard you in all your ways."

Again, the ministry of angels is continually occurring, though we're not aware of what's happening. What we think are ordinary coincidences are oftentimes the result of the ministry of angels.

In the beginning of the war, the Royal Air Force (RAF) constantly flew missions against Germany and attacked the bombers headed for England. This understaffed group of courageous pilots often flew beyond their physical limits of endurance with equipment that was mechanically unfit to fly.

After the war, Chief Air Marshal Lloyd Hugh Dowding attended a victory celebration. In the presence of royalty, the Prime Minister and many dignitaries, he told of fliers who, having been hit by enemy fire, were either incapacitated or dead. *Yet, their planes kept on flying and fighting.* On occasion, British pilots would see a figure still operating the controls. Mr. Dowding said he believed angels had actually flown some of the planes whose pilots sat dead in their cockpits.[1]

An Angel to the Rescue

On October 3, 1984, a flight engineer on a restored World War II Navy PBY (amphibious seaplane) was settling into his flight engineer seat in the "conning" tower. This is the compartment between the fuselage and the wings that's just big enough for one person. It has two small side windows, and the entire front is walled in with instruments and controls.

On this early morning flight off the coast of Texas near Harlingen, with ten people on board, the pilot misjudged the distance over the waters of the Gulf of Mexico on a low pass and hit the surf in a nose-down position.

The nose gear doors suddenly ripped open, serving as a speed brake on the water. The rush of water caused the plane to explode; the engines and propellers ripped off their mounts and continued their forward momentum. The cockpit completely separated from the rest of the plane and rolled under water as the tail section sheared off and rose into the air like a giant whale. All of this happened in seconds with no warning.

The flight engineer blacked out and awoke in his dark compartment, with only his head above the water and fuel that poured down, filling the compartment. Perched precariously above him were the wing and fuel tanks, containing more than three hundred gallons of gasoline. "All I could think of was that this was the end and I was going to die," he recalls. He began to pray and think about his wife and daughters.

Suddenly, he noticed a bright glow to his left, where no light should have been on an overcast morning. He somehow followed this mysterious glow (later realizing it signaled the only means of passage out of the wreck) and swam underwater to safety. The next thing he knew, he was sitting alone on top of the floating wing and above the compartment.

There wasn't another person around, nor a sound to be heard. Tragically, only three of the passengers and crew survived. They stayed on the wreckage until fishermen hauled them to shore, where they were taken to a hospital for treatment.[2]

Angels in Action

Along with the stories of personal experience I've recorded in this book, there are so many stories in the Bible regarding the activity of angels. In the next chapter, I've selected a handful of stories that illustrate angels as mighty ministering spirits. Some of them we've already mentioned, but I've provided the full details of the biblical story here.

Some may be familiar to you, although I hope you'll enjoy reviewing them in the reader-friendly translation of *The Message*, by Eugene Peterson. My hope is that each story will renew your appreciation for the work of God's spirit servants, the angels.

---

[1] Graham, Angels, 164.

[2] As told by Jerry Gardner.

CHAPTER SEVEN

Famous Angels in the Bible

As we study Scripture, we find that angels have an interesting ministry in announcing the birth of babies. The first time we encounter angels in the Bible is in the Book of Genesis. An angel appeared to Abram and Sarai's maidservant, named Hagar, with an important message about the baby she was carrying.

Although God had promised Sarai and Abram their own child, Sarai was still barren. In her old age, she had tried to manipulate her circumstances by suggesting Hagar serve as a surrogate mother. The story begins this way:

[1]Sarai, Abram's wife, hadn't yet produced a child.

She had an Egyptian maid named Hagar. [2]Sarai said to
Abram, "GOD has not seen fit to let me have a child. Sleep
with my maid. Maybe I can get a family from her." Abram
agreed to do what Sarai said.

[3]So Sarai, Abram's wife, took her Egyptian maid Hagar
and gave her to her husband Abram as a wife. Abram had
been living ten years in Canaan when this took place. [4]He
slept with Hagar and she got pregnant. When she learned
she was pregnant, she looked down on her mistress.

[5]Sarai told Abram, "It's all your fault that I'm suffering this abuse. I put my maid in bed with you and the minute she knows she's pregnant, she treats me like I'm nothing. May GOD decide which of us is right."

[6]"You decide," said Abram. "Your maid is your business."

Sarai was abusive to Hagar and she ran away.

[7]An angel of GOD found her beside a spring in the
desert; it was the spring on the road to Shur. [8]He said,
"Hagar, maid of Sarai, what are you doing here?"

She said, "I'm running away from Sarai my mistress."

[9]The angel of GOD said, "Go back to your mistress. Put
up with her abuse." [10]He continued, "I'm going to give you
a big family, children past counting.

[11]From this pregnancy, you'll get a son: Name him Ishmael;
for GOD heard you, GOD answered you.
[12]He'll be a bucking bronco of a man,
a real fighter, fighting and being fought,
Always stirring up trouble,
always at odds with his family."

[13]She answered GOD by name, praying to the God who spoke to her,
"You're the God who sees me!"
"Yes! He saw me; and then I saw him!"
(Genesis 16:1–13 – *The Message*)

As we'll see later on in this chapter, a group of angels appeared soon afterward to Abram and Sarai to announce the imminent birth of a son of their own.

An angel also appeared to Manoah, the father of Samson, and told him and his wife they'd be parents of a son (Judges 13:3). This angel even prescribed a special diet for the mother of Samson to eat during her pregnancy.

And an angel appeared to Zachariah, the father of John the Baptist, to announce the birth of that child. Could it be that some of these angels are "obstetric angels" because they're so interested in the birth of babies? Of course, the most celebrated birth of all came accompanied by angels—the birth of the Messiah, Jesus Christ.

Angels at the Birth of Jesus

When Joseph discovered that Mary, his fiancée, was pregnant, he had an emotionally charged decision to make. He had a choice of legal options. One was to follow a prescribed ceremony to shame her publicly. Another possibility was to have her publicly stoned, an acceptable legal right at the time. (You may recall the story, in John 8:1–11, of the woman caught in adultery who was brought before Jesus to be stoned.

Joseph, however, decided he would do neither of those things. Rather, he would just put her away quietly. Fortunately, an angel came to Joseph in a dream and changed his mind. The Bible tells the rest of the story:

[18]The birth of Jesus took place like this. His mother, Mary,
was engaged to be married to Joseph. Before they came to
the marriage bed, Joseph discovered she was pregnant. (It
was by the Holy Spirit, but he didn't know that.) [19]Joseph,
chagrined but noble, determined to take care of things
quietly so Mary would not be disgraced.

[20]While he was trying to figure a way out, he had a
dream. God's angel spoke in the dream: "Joseph, son of
David, don't hesitate to get married. Mary's pregnancy is
Spirit-conceived. God's Holy Spirit has made her pregnant.
[21]She will bring a son to birth, and when she does, you,
Joseph, will name him Jesus—'God saves'—because he
will save his people from their sins." [22]This would bring the
prophet's embryonic sermon to full term:

[23]Watch for this—a virgin will get pregnant and
bear a son;

They will name him Emmanuel (Hebrew for "God is with us").

[24]Then Joseph woke up. He did exactly what God's angel commanded in the dream: He married Mary. [25]But he did not consummate the marriage until she had the baby. He named the baby Jesus.
(Matthew 1:18–25, *The Message*)

And from the gospel of Luke, we have the announcement from the angel Gabriel himself:

[26]In the sixth month of Elizabeth's pregnancy, God sent the angel Gabriel to the Galilean village of Nazareth [27]to a virgin engaged to be married to a man descended from David. His name was Joseph, and the virgin's name, Mary.
[28]Upon entering, Gabriel greeted her:

"Good morning!
You're beautiful with God's beauty,
Beautiful inside and out!
God be with you."

[29]She was thoroughly shaken, wondering what was behind a greeting like that. [30]But the angel assured her, "Mary, you have nothing to fear. God has a surprise for you:
[31]You will become pregnant and give birth to a son and call his name Jesus.

[32]He will be great,
be called 'Son of the Highest.'
The Lord God will give him
the throne of his father David;
[33]He will rule Jacob's house forever—
no end, ever, to his kingdom."

[34]Mary said to the angel, "But how? I've never slept with a man."

[35]The angel answered,
"The Holy Spirit will come upon you,

the power of the Highest hover over you;
Therefore, the child you bring to birth
will be called Holy, Son of God.
36"And did you know that your cousin Elizabeth
conceived a son, old as she is? Everyone called her barren,
and here she is six months pregnant! 37Nothing, you see, is
impossible with God."
38And Mary said,
"Yes, I see it all now:
I'm the Lord's maid, ready to serve.
Let it be with me
just as you say."
Then the angel left her.
(Luke 1:26–38, *The Message*)

Consider the following riddle: Who was the only baby born who was older than his mother and the same age as his daddy? Do you know the answer? Jesus Christ. He was older than His mother. Jesus said, "Before Abraham was, I Am" (John 8:58).

Jesus Christ has always existed in the form of God, the Son. He was the same age as His father because His father was God Almighty. Mary was the mother of Jesus, but Joseph was not the biological father of Jesus. He took care of Jesus, but God was the Father of the Lord Jesus Christ.

The first place we see angels operating in the life of Jesus was when they announced the divine components of His birth. The virgin birth of Jesus Christ is not some incidental doctrine of our faith; it is absolutely essential to the deity of Jesus Christ. And an angel was there to certify it happened exactly the way God designed.

Entertaining Angels Unaware

Remember the writer of Hebrews' admonition about the importance of being kind to strangers (13:2)? Some people, like Abraham and Sarah in the following story, have unknowingly entertained angels that appeared to them as mysterious strangers. Consider their account:

[1]GOD appeared to Abraham at the Oaks of Mamre while he was sitting at the entrance of his tent. It was the hottest part of the day. [2]He looked up and saw three men standing. He ran from his tent to greet them and bowed before them.

[3]He said, "Master, if it please you, stop for a while with your servant. [4]I'll get some water so you can wash your feet. Rest under this tree. [5]I'll get some food to refresh you on your way, since your travels have brought you across my path."

They said, "Certainly. Go ahead."

[6]Abraham hurried into the tent to Sarah. He said, "Hurry. Get three cups of our best flour; knead it and make bread."

[7]Then Abraham ran to the cattle pen and picked out a nice plump calf and gave it to the servant who lost no time getting it ready. [8]Then he got curds and milk, brought them with the calf that had been roasted, set the meal before the men, and stood there under the tree while they ate.

[9]The men said to him, "Where is Sarah your wife?"

He said, "In the tent."

[10]One of them said, "I'm coming back about this time next year. When I arrive, your wife Sarah will have a son." Sarah was listening at the tent opening, just behind the man.

[11]Abraham and Sarah were old by this time, very old. Sarah was far past the age for having babies. [12]Sarah laughed within herself, "An old woman like me? Get pregnant? With this old man of a husband?"

[13]GOD said to Abraham, "Why did Sarah laugh saying, 'Me? Have a baby? An old woman like me?' [14]Is anything too hard for GOD? I'll be back about this time next year and Sarah will have a baby."

[15]Sarah lied. She said, "I didn't laugh," because she was afraid.

But he said, "Yes you did; you laughed." [16]When the men got up to leave, they set off for Sodom. Abraham walked with them to say good-bye.
(Genesis 18:1–16, *The Message*)

Mystery Men Come into Town

The story of the mysterious strangers continues in the next chapter of Genesis, as they made their way toward Sodom (and nearby Gomorrah), wicked cities with notorious reputations. The angels were there to save the one righteous citizen of Sodom—Lot—and his family, and to destroy all those who remained. However, as we'll see, neither Lot nor the evil men of Sodom recognized these angels-on-mission until it was almost too late.

[1]The two angels arrived at Sodom in the evening. Lot was sitting at the city gate. He saw them and got up to welcome them, bowing before them [2]and said, "Please, my friends, come to my house and stay the night. Wash up. You can rise early and be on your way refreshed."

They said, "No, we'll sleep in the street."

[3]But he insisted, wouldn't take no for an answer; and they relented and went home with him. Lot fixed a hot meal for them and they ate.

[4]Before they went to bed men from all over the city of Sodom, young and old, descended on the house from all sides and boxed them in. [5]They yelled to Lot, "Where are the men who are staying with you for the night? Bring them out so we can have our sport with them!"

[6]Lot went out, barring the door behind him, [7]and said, "Brothers, please, don't be vile! [8]Look, I have two daughters, virgins; let me bring them out; you can take your pleasure with them, but don't touch these men—they're my guests."

[9]They said, "Get lost! You drop in from nowhere and now you're going to tell us how to run our lives. We'll treat

you worse than them!" And they charged past Lot to break
down the door.

10But the two men reached out and pulled Lot inside the
house, locking the door. 11Then they struck blind the men
who were trying to break down the door, both leaders and
followers, leaving them groping in the dark.

12The two men said to Lot, "Do you have any other
family here? Sons, daughters—anybody in the city? Get
them out of here, and now! 13We're going to destroy this
place. The outcries of victims here to GOD are deafening;
we've been sent to blast this place into oblivion."

14Lot went out and warned the fiancés of his daughters,
"Evacuate this place; GOD is about to destroy this city!"
But his daughters' would-be husbands treated it as a joke.

15At break of day, the angels pushed Lot to get going,
"Hurry. Get your wife and two daughters out of here
before it's too late and you're caught in the punishment of
the city."

16Lot was dragging his feet. The men grabbed Lot's
arm, and the arms of his wife and daughters—GOD was so
merciful to them!—and dragged them to safety outside the
city. 17When they had them outside, Lot was told, "Now run
for your life! Don't look back! Don't stop anywhere on the
plain—run for the hills or you'll be swept away."

18But Lot protested, "No, masters, you can't mean it! 19I
know that you've taken a liking to me and have done me an
immense favor in saving my life, but I can't run for the
mountains—who knows what terrible thing might happen to
me in the mountains and leave me for dead. 20Look over
there—that town is close enough to get to. It's a small town,
hardly anything to it. Let me escape there and save my
life—it's a mere wide place in the road."

21He said to him, "All right. If you insist. I'll let you
have your way. And I won't stamp out the town you've spot-
ted. 22But hurry up. Run for it! I can't do anything until you

get there." That's why the town was called Zoar, that is,
Smalltown.
23The sun was high in the sky when Lot arrived at Zoar.
24Then GOD rained brimstone and fire down on Sodom
and Gomorrah—a river of lava from GOD out of the sky!—
25and destroyed these cities and the entire plain and everyone who lived in the cities and everything that grew from
the ground.
26But Lot's wife looked back and turned into a pillar
of salt.
27Abraham got up early the next morning and went to
the place he had so recently stood with GOD. 28He looked
out over Sodom and Gomorrah, surveying the whole plain.
All he could see was smoke belching from the Earth, like
smoke from a furnace.
29And that's the story: When God destroyed the Cities of
the Plain, he was mindful of Abraham and first got Lot out of
there before he blasted those cities off the face of the Earth.
(Genesis 19:1–29, *The Message*)

"O GOD, Open His Eyes..."

In answer to the question, "Are we really alone?" we have this story tucked away in the book of 2 Kings. When the prophet Elisha and his servant faced off with an enemy fighting force, they must have felt dreadfully alone and entirely abandoned. But were they really alone?

8One time when the king of Aram was at war with Israel,
after consulting with his officers, he said, "At such and
such a place I want an ambush set." 9The Holy Man sent a
message to the king of Israel: "Watch out when you're
passing this place, because Aram has set an ambush there."
10So the king of Israel sent word concerning the place of
which the Holy Man had warned him. This kind of thing
happened all the time.

11 The king of Aram was furious over all this. He called his officers together and said, “Tell me, who is leaking information to the king of Israel? Who is the spy in our ranks?”

12 But one of his men said, “No, my master, dear king. It’s not any of us. It’s Elisha the prophet in Israel. He tells the king of Israel everything you say, even what you whisper in your bedroom.”

13 The king said, “Go and find out where he is. I’ll send someone and capture him.”

The report came back, “He’s in Dothan.”

14 Then he dispatched horses and chariots, an impressive fighting force. They came by night and surrounded the city.

15 Early in the morning a servant of the Holy Man got up and went out. Surprise! Horses and chariots surrounding the city! The young man exclaimed, “Oh, master! What shall we do?”

16 He said, “Don’t worry about it—there are more on our side than on their side.”

17 Then Elisha prayed, “O GOD, open his eyes and let him see.”

The eyes of the young man were opened and he saw. A wonder! The whole mountainside full of horses and chariots of fire surrounding Elisha!

18 When the Arameans attacked, Elisha prayed to GOD, “Strike these people blind!” And GOD struck them blind, just as Elisha said.

19 Then Elisha called out to them, “Not that way! Not this city! Follow me and I’ll lead you to the man you’re looking for.” And he led them into Samaria.

20 As they entered the city, Elisha prayed, “O GOD, open their eyes so they can see where they are.” GOD opened their eyes. They looked around—they were trapped in Samaria!

21 When the king of Israel saw them, he said to Elisha, “Father, shall I massacre the lot?”

[22]"Not on your life!" said Elisha. "You didn't lift a hand to capture them, and now you're going to kill them? No sir, make a feast for them and send them back to their master."

[23]So he prepared a huge feast for them. After they ate and drank their fill he dismissed them. Then they returned home to their master. The raiding bands of Aram didn't bother Israel anymore.
(2 Kings 6:8–23, *The Message*)

Climbing Jacob's Ladder

As children, we used to sing, "We are climbing Jacob's ladder." Although you can't get into heaven by climbing Jacob's ladder—it's marked "Angels Only"—angels move back and forth between earthly and heavenly realms with ease. Read how the Bible describes it:

[10]Jacob left Beersheba and went to Haran. [11]He came to a certain place and camped for the night since the sun had set. He took one of the stones there, set it under his head and lay down to sleep. [12]And he dreamed: A stairway was set on the ground and it reached all the way to the sky; angels of God were going up and going down on it.

[13]Then GOD was right before him, saying, "I am GOD, the God of Abraham your father and the God of Isaac. I'm giving the ground on which you are sleeping to you and to your descendants. [14]Your descendants will be as the dust of the Earth; they'll stretch from west to east and from north to south. All the families of the Earth will bless themselves in you and your descendants. [15]Yes. I'll stay with you, I'll protect you wherever you go, and I'll bring you back to this very ground. I'll stick with you until I've done everything I promised you."

[16]Jacob woke up from his sleep. He said, "GOD is in this place—truly. And I didn't even know it!" [17]He was terrified. He whispered in awe, "Incredible. Wonderful.

Holy. This is God's House. This is the Gate of Heaven." (Genesis 28:10–17, *The Message*)

Elijah Encounters a Gourmet Angel

Is there such a thing as a "gourmet angel"? Read the account of how Elijah regained his second wind after a run for his life and decide for yourself:

[1]Ahab reported to Jezebel everything that Elijah had done, including the massacre of the prophets. [2]Jezebel immediately sent a messenger to Elijah with her threat: "The gods will get you for this and I'll get even with you! By this time tomorrow you'll be as dead as any one of those prophets."

[3]When Elijah saw how things were, he ran for dear life to Beersheba, far in the south of Judah. He left his young servant there [4]and then went on into the desert another day's journey. He came to a lone broom bush and collapsed in its shade, wanting in the worst way to be done with it all—to just die: "Enough of this, GOD! Take my life—I'm ready to join my ancestors in the grave!" [5]Exhausted, he fell asleep under the lone broom bush.

Suddenly an angel shook him awake and said, "Get up and eat!"

[6]He looked around and, to his surprise, right by his head were a loaf of bread baked on some coals and a jug of water. He ate the meal and went back to sleep.

[7]The angel of GOD came back, shook him awake again, and said, "Get up and eat some more—you've got a long journey ahead of you."

[8]He got up, ate and drank his fill, and set out. Nourished by that meal, he walked forty days and nights, all the way to the mountain of God, to Horeb.
(1 Kings 19:1–8, *The Message*)

Angels at the Resurrection of Jesus

After Jesus died, He was buried in a tomb provided by Joseph of Arimathea. The reason the stone in front of the tomb was rolled away was not because Jesus needed an exit cleared. The stone was moved for our benefit, not His. God wanted us to look into the tomb and see that it was empty.

I can imagine that a powerful angel effortlessly wrestled that stone away from the entrance to the tomb, sat on top of it, crossed his legs and waited for the women who were the first to visit Jesus' tomb on Sunday. The Bible recalls the extraordinary events of that fantastic day:

[1]After the Sabbath, as the first light of the new week dawned, Mary Magdalene and the other Mary came to keep vigil at the tomb. [2]Suddenly the earth reeled and rocked under their feet as God's angel came down from heaven, came right up to where they were standing. He rolled back the stone and then sat on it. [3]Shafts of lightning blazed from him. His garments shimmered snow-white.

[4]The guards at the tomb were scared to death. They were so frightened, they couldn't move.

[5]The angel spoke to the women: "There is nothing to fear here. I know you're looking for Jesus, the One they nailed to the cross. [6]He is not here. He was raised, just as he said. Come and look at the place where he was placed.

[7]"Now, get on your way quickly and tell his disciples, 'He is risen from the dead. He is going on ahead of you to Galilee. You will see him there.' That's the message."

[8]The women, deep in wonder and full of joy, lost no time in leaving the tomb. They ran to tell the disciples. (Matthew 28:1–8, *The Message*)

Do Angels Still Help Us Today?

Some of you may be thinking, "These are great angel stories. But that was a long time ago—does God still use angels like that today?" The title of an earlier book I wrote about angels ten years ago posed the question, "*Do Angels Really Exist?*" I received many requests for interviews on radio programs (both religious and secular) to discuss the facts and fantasies surrounding angels. However, simply believing angels exist isn't enough. Yes, angels really do exist. But there's more to it than that. There is a *reason* angels still exist today.

CHAPTER EIGHT

How Angels Help Us

Each winter, hundreds of skiing enthusiasts trade their sandals for ski boots and head from Los Angeles to the snowy mountains in Big Bear, California. It's a short three-hour drive from the beach, but snow chains are often required to reach the mountaintops through the winding pass. Record snowstorms have sometimes closed off the tiny resort town of Big Bear to incoming and outgoing traffic, stranding residents and guests in an unlikely winter wonderland a few thousand feet above L.A.

One longtime resident of Big Bear recalls making her way into town after a heavy snowfall from her mountainside cabin. "My children, father and I were slowly driving down the street from the cabin and using our snow chains to plow through the thick snow. As we neared an intersection at the top of a steep hill, the car hit a patch of ice and suddenly began careening off the side of the road and into a deep embankment. I gripped the steering wheel and pumped the brakes to no avail.

"Everything happened so fast, but it seemed like slow motion as I tried to figure out how to keep the car from crashing into the ditch. The kids were terrified and everyone panicked. Thankfully, Daddy spoke up just in time with an idea, 'Put the car in reverse,' he said in a voice that surprised me with its calm demeanor. I did so, and immediately the car came to a halt, teetering near the edge of the embankment below. We caught our breath and sighed with relief.

"'How did you know to do that?' I asked him, still shaking from the adrenaline.

"'Do what?' my dad said.

"'You told me to put the car in reverse—how did you know that would work?'

"'I didn't say anything,' Daddy insisted. 'I was just as scared as you were.'

"In the midst of our fear, I know I had heard a voice, clear and commanding, instructing me what to do. To this day, I believe an angel spoke those words to me and kept us from danger."[1]

In Exodus 23:20, God said to Moses, "See, I am sending an angel ahead of you to guard you along the way and to bring you to the place I have prepared." I've received many stories of angel encounters and the majority of them deal with God's supernatural protection. Most of the accounts are of events that occurred when people were driving.

That's interesting, in light of the fact that motor vehicle crashes are one of the leading causes of death and injury every year. We're more at risk each time we're on the road than perhaps at any other time. People can recall near misses on the road that happened thirty or forty years ago. They haven't been able to forget these encounters, because they believe God's angels were there to protect them.

Many people would say they believe there are angels; they may even appreciate their existence. They just don't know why they exist and what purpose they serve. They may see signs of heaven on earth—but why? Why did God create a special company of heavenly beings? We just can't fully appreciate these beings until we recognize that they have a specific purpose and define what that purpose is. Like the angel in this story, a major role of angels is to guard and protect us. But angels exist to do much more.

When We Face Temptation

Jesus' earthly ministry is bracketed by two times of intense temptation. The Bible makes a point of recording the details of the situations, and it also makes note of the fact that each time angels came and helped Him through it. Of course, we can assume Jesus experienced all kinds of temptation beyond these two instances recorded for our benefit.

Temptation in the Desert

Matthew 4:1–3 declares, "Then Jesus was led by the Spirit into the desert to be tempted by the devil. After fasting forty days and forty nights, he was hungry. The tempter came to him and said, 'If you are the Son of God, tell these stones to become bread.'" Three times the devil tempted Him, and three times Jesus overcame the temptation (see Matthew 4:1–10).

Scripture says in Hebrews that Jesus was tempted at every point, just as we are. Yet He never sinned. Everyone battles temptation. The way Jesus resisted temptation is the same way we resist temptation. Three times, Jesus drew the Word of God as a sword and responded to the devil's temptation by quoting Scripture. Three times, He said, "It is written."

The best way for us to overcome temptation is to have the Word of God hidden in our hearts. We don't memorize Scripture so we can impress other people or show how much we know. We memorize Scripture so we can stay clean before the Lord. The Bible says, "Thy word have I hid in my heart that I might not sin against thee" (Psalm 119:11, KJV).

After Jesus was victorious over His temptation, something else happened. Sometimes we forget this part of the experience. "Then the devil left him, and angels came and attended him" (Matthew 4:11). The King James Bible says they "ministered unto him." The word *ministered* or *attended* is the Greek word *diakoneo*, from which we get our word *deacon*—a leader whose role is to minister and to care for others in the church.

That word *ministering* or *attending* could mean they fed Him a meal, as with Elijah (1 Kings 19:5–8). Jesus was hungry, after all. He'd been without food for forty days and forty nights. Perhaps the angels ministered to Jesus in that very specific way.

Can angels minister to us in a similar way they did to Jesus? Certainly they can. The angels don't know what it's like to experience temptation, but they know we do. And they're there to minister to us when we undergo it.

Temptation in the Garden

Toward the end of His earthly ministry, Jesus faced another great temptation in the Garden of Gethsemane. The cross loomed large in front of Him, and He was tempted to take the easy way out. He said, "My Father, if it is possible, may this cup be taken from me. Yet, not as I will, but as you will" (Matthew 26:39).

The Bible says He faced that temptation, overcame it and committed Himself to the cross—despite being in such mental, emotional and spiritual anguish that His sweat appeared as drops of blood on the ground (Luke 22:44).

At that moment of great resolve, Scripture says an angel came and ministered to Him. "An angel from heaven appeared to him and strengthened him" (Luke 22:43). Perhaps the angel whispered encouragement to Jesus and wiped his bloody brow. We don't really know how the angel served Him, but when Jesus needed a touch from His Father, God sent an angel in the nick of time.

Angels in Our Everyday Lives

Whenever we think of angels ministering to our needs, we may think of supernatural situations like the ones we've already described. However, sometimes an angel touches us in very common, ordinary experiences.

A woman once wrote to me about her twin sons—very active little boys. She related that one Sunday morning she was trying to get them ready for Sunday school—harder than it sounds when there are two of them! When she got one boy cleaned up and dressed, she set him to the side and started working on the second one.

While she was dressing him, the first one somehow wormed his way under the bathroom sink. When the exasperated mother turned around, she saw a once neatly-dressed boy covered in grease and dripping wet—but perfectly pleased with himself.

While she turned to deal with him, the second boy squirmed out of her reach and found his way outside, where he promptly jumped in the dirt. She said she finally wrangled both of them in front of her, and was about to lose her temper. Naturally, she was tempted to scream and execute judgment on them at that moment, but instead she said aloud, "Get thee behind me, Satan."

She said that once she resisted the temptation to lose her temper, it was as if she could feel somebody putting hands on her arms from behind and saying, "Settle down. Take it easy. Everything is going to be okay."

I think that sometimes when we resist temptation, the angels do for us what they did for the Lord Jesus Christ: they help us at our point of need. The next time you're facing temptation, listen for the silent words of encouragement, "Steady now." Pay attention for the possibility of unseen arms to restrain you.

What's the Difference between Angels and the Holy Spirit?

As I teach about angels, God's ministering spirits, I'm often asked, "What's the difference between angels, God's ministering spirits, and the Holy Spirit? Why doesn't God just do everything through the Holy Spirit?"

I don't claim to understand all the mysteries of the Scriptures. There are certain unfathomable truths about the person of God and the reality of angels that we can never figure out. The Bible teaches that the Holy Spirit comes to live inside every Christian. To the disciples, Jesus said, "Receive the Holy Spirit" (John 20:22). To the multitude who gathered with Him just before the Ascension, He said, "But you will receive power when the Holy Spirit comes on you" (Acts 1:8).

The Bible explains that God gives the Holy Spirit to every believer. "Those who obey his commands live in him, and he in them. And this is how we know that he lives in us: We know it by the Spirit he gave us" (1 John 3:24). Paul, too, says it clearly, "Because you are sons, God sent the Spirit of his Son into our hearts, the Spirit who calls out, "*Abba*, Father" (Galatians 4:6). And again he writes to the Corinthians, "Do you not know that your body is a temple of the Holy Spirit, who is in you, whom you have received from God? You are not your own" (1 Corinthians 6:19).

The verb used in this verse is also used most often to describe the unique relationship God initiates through His Spirit. It actually comes from the Greek word for house—*oikos*. It means "to live in," "reside," or "dwell." *Oikeo* is used three other times to describe our relationship with the Holy Spirit (see Romans 8:9, 11; 1 Corinthians 3:16; 2 Timothy 1:14).

To the contrary, angels never live inside a person. Jesus said of the Holy Spirit, "And I will ask the Father, and he will give you another Counselor to be with you forever—the

Spirit of truth. The world cannot accept him, because it neither sees him nor knows him. But you know him, for he lives with you and will be in you" (John 14:16–17). The Holy Spirit, unlike angels, takes up residence in the heart of every believer.

The Holy Spirit Speaks

One of the purposes for the Holy Spirit living inside us is to speak to us from the Father. Some reader may be thinking right now, "I'm not too sure about this. Does the Holy Spirit actually speak?"

Certainly He does. Consider the example in Acts where Peter received a vision from God while he was praying on a rooftop. "While Peter was still thinking about the vision, the Spirit said to him, 'Simon, three men are looking for you. So, get up and go downstairs. Do not hesitate to go with them, for I have sent them'" (Acts 10:19–20).

Most Christians I know confirm that in these days of the completed New Testament, when the Holy Spirit does speak to us, He doesn't use an audible voice. Instead, He speaks to receptive hearts. Sometimes when we're trying to determine God's will in a particular matter, it's the intercession of the Holy Spirit from the Father to you that reveals His will. The Bible explains it this way:

> In the same way, the Spirit helps us in our weakness. We do not know what we ought to pray, but the Spirit himself intercedes for us with groans that words cannot express. And he who searches our hearts knows the mind of the Spirit, because the Spirit intercedes for the saints in accordance with God's will. (Romans 8:26–27)

While angels, God's ministering spirits sent to serve the saints, may come and go on an as-needed basis, God's Spirit never leaves you. He lives inside you and is there with you wherever you go. Jesus assured us of that fact when He said, "My sheep listen to my voice; I know them, and they follow me. I give them eternal life, and they shall never perish; no one can snatch them out of my hand. My Father, who has given them to me, is greater than all; no one can snatch them out of my Father's hand" (John 10:27–29).

Touched by an Angel

The Holy Spirit attends to us spiritually, whereas God gives angels the unique authority to minister to us physically. Remember the example of Elijah's encounter in 1 Kings 19? Elijah felt the same way many of us feel sometimes—physically exhausted, emotionally drained and spiritually depleted. God sent an angel to minister to Elijah's physical needs. He went to sleep and the angel came and poked Elijah in the ribs and encouraged him to eat and gain his strength.

The Bible never says the Holy Spirit can actually touch a person physically, but angels can and do. The Bible says the food the angel prepared was a cake. (What kind of cake? Obviously, angel food cake!)

In Psalm 78:25, we read, "Men ate the bread of angels; he sent them all the food they could eat." This is referring to the manna God provided each day for the children of Israel in the wilderness. There's something about the nature and ministry of angels that demonstrates their ability to attend to our physical needs, even in terms of providing food.

I once talked with a very well-respected widow who shared with me about a time she believed an angel ministered to her. After the death of her husband, it was extremely difficult for her to work through her grief. She said it seemed as if she couldn't stop crying. She had never realized just how big, cold and empty a bed could be until her husband died.

One night she was in bed, lying on her side. She was crying and praying, saying, "Oh, God, when will it end? When will the pain end?" At that moment, she said she felt arms wrap around and lovingly embrace her from behind. She added that she was afraid to look, but those arms were as real as any arms she had ever felt.

She slept peacefully that night, which was the beginning of her peace and victory over that time of grief. She told me she believes it was an angel of God sent to help her, even giving her physical comfort at that time.

In Genesis 32:24, we read about the night when Jacob physically wrestled with a being who is called a man, but who is obviously an angel armed with supernatural strength. Indeed, angels can physically touch us.

Do You Have a Guardian Angel?

In Psalm 34:7, we read: "The angel of the Lord encamps around those who fear him, and he delivers them." Recall God's promise in Psalm 91, "If you make the Most High your dwelling—even the Lord, who is my refuge—then no harm will befall you, no disaster will come near your tent. For he will command his angels concerning you to guard you in all your ways; they will lift you up in their hands, so that you will not strike your foot against a stone" (vv. 9–12). So, is there such a thing as a guardian angel?

Many people speak of having a guardian angel, and some churches teach that individuals have one with them from birth until death, never leaving them. Some churches even teach people to pray regularly to their guardian angels.

What do the Scriptures say on this subject? Nothing! It's not taught anywhere in the Bible, nor is the phrase "guardian angel" even mentioned. The closest thing to it is in Matthew 18:10, where Jesus is speaking about little children. "See that you do not look down on one of these little ones. For I tell you that their angels in heaven always see the face of my Father in heaven."

Many people have greatly misunderstood this verse and taken it as proof that there's a "guardian angel" assigned to every child, and perhaps to every Christian, regardless of age. Jesus taught that children have angels who are interested in their care. However, if we try to find Scripture to substantiate the teaching that one angel accompanies us all our lives, we will be disappointed.

I don't believe in a singular guardian angel, but I do believe in the reality of *many* guardian angels—which is far better. God sends the host of His angels to guard us and to keep us from hurting ourselves at times. In fact, this multitude of angels forms an impenetrable barrier of protection. The Bible uses the picture of a hedge of protection to describe God's watchful care for us.

When We Need Protection

The story of missionaries John Pollock and his wife who went to the New Hebrides Islands in the South Pacific illustrates angelic protection.[2] When they arrived, they were the first Anglo people the natives had ever seen. The tribal magician feared these white intruders, so he convinced the members of his tribe that these strangers had come to kill their children.

On the evening of their arrival, the natives surrounded the hut of John and his wife, planning to storm it and kill them. Expecting to be attacked at any moment, the Pollocks stayed on their knees praying for safety all through the night. The night passed and the native warriors never came any closer.

Gradually, the Pollocks learned the local language and soon won the trust of the people. Many of them even came to know Christ. After the chief of the tribe became a Christian, John asked him about that night long ago when his tribe had surrounded their hut. To John's amazement, the chief said he had never ordered the attack because a host of large men, encamped around the hut, swords in hand, had kept them at bay.

In his book on angels, Billy Graham suggests this, too, was an example of a modern manifestation of God's special secret agents—His angels who served as a hedge of protection.

A Hedge About Us

When you hear the word "hedge," what you think of? Most people think of a hedge made of plants. You may have a set of hedge clippers somewhere in your garage that you use to trim plants. But the word "hedge" in the Bible describes something more substantial than a bush.

The Hebrew word means a "wall" and brings to mind a protective fence, a barrier. A hedge was a defensive wall often built around a city. The bottom part might be comprised of stones or hard packed dirt, and there might be thorny plants on the top of it. God's hedge is not a hedge of stones or a hedge of plants; it's a hedge of angels.

Recall the story of Job. In his conversation with God, Satan pointed out that God had built a spiritual "hedge" around Job, around his family (household) and around all his possessions. God can provide a spiritual barrier around His servants to protect them from spiritual attacks. Job couldn't see the hedge, but Satan could. Remember, many things that exist in the spiritual world are invisible to our eyes, but that doesn't mean they aren't real—they are.

God's hedge of protection around His servants is part of His promise, and can only be removed by his permission. The great Bible teacher, Dr. J. Vernon McGee, had a radio broadcast for many years called, "Through the Bible." In Dr. McGee's commentary on Job, he confirms the hedge of protection around every believer. In fact, anything that touches your life, explains McGee, must first be permitted and then ultimately used for God's purposes.[3]

Praying for Protection

Did you know you can pray for a hedge of protection around those you love? Parents and grandparents should pray for a hedge of protection around their children and grandchildren. Friends should pray for friends, and families for other families. As the following story illustrates, we never know when we'll need God's protection.

A young woman and her husband were traveling back late one evening from a weekend of camping. On this particular leg of the journey, the wife took over driving while the husband slept. Slowed by a large truck in front of her, the woman tried again and again to pass it—carefully veering over the lane to see if the way ahead was clear. When she decided it was safe to begin to pass, she pulled out.

Suddenly, her husband's hand flashed in front of her face, pointing his finger toward a car that had been traveling in her blind spot. She hadn't seen the car and turned to thank her husband for pointing it out. However, when she looked over in the passenger seat, her husband was still fast asleep. Whose hand had protected her from certain disaster? She believes it was one of God's angels.

Husbands and wives can also pray for God to put a hedge around their mate—not only for physical protection, but emotional protection as well. This particular prayer is illustrated in the story of Hosea and Gomer in the Old Testament. The entire story is an allegory of how Israel tried to be unfaithful to God.

Hosea's wife, Gomer, was an adulteress. When she wandered away from her husband, God set up a "hedge" to keep her from being unfaithful to Hosea.

God says about Gomer (who represents wayward Israel), "Therefore I will block her path with thornbushes; I will wall her in so that she cannot find her way. She will chase after her lovers but not catch them...Then she will say, 'I will go back to my husband as at first, for I was better off than now'" (Hosea 2:6–7). If your mate is working or traveling in an area where there's sexual temptation, you should pray for God to hedge him or her in with His holy angels.

Where Was an Angel When I Needed One?

As you read about how angels protect us from harm, you may have reflected upon your own experiences and thought about a loved one—a believer who had an accident and God didn't seem to protect him or her. Why wasn't that person protected? You may wonder, "Where were the angels when my loved one or my friend suffered and died?"

I don't understand it; all I know is that sometimes angels are there to protect and sometimes they aren't. According to God's sovereign will, He sometimes allows good people to suffer and die.

If you really struggle, write down this Scripture reference, Hebrews 11:35. Chapter 11 of Hebrews tells about all the great saints of God, "the roll call of faith," and how God supernaturally delivered many. The last part of the passage, however, tells about all those God *did not* supernaturally deliver.

There were those who suffered from the sword and were cut in half, stoned and died terrible, painful deaths. Then it gives a hint of explanation why this happened: "...so that they might gain a better resurrection" (11:35).

It's wonderful to be protected supernaturally and to be delivered, but in God's mysterious plan, sometimes it's even better for Christians to go and be with Jesus. Paul said, "For to me, to live is Christ and to die is gain" (Philippians 1:21). On some occasions, the angels are there, but God's will for them is to carry that person's soul and spirit into heaven.

Another of the angels' primary roles is to peacefully preside at our deaths. More on this in a later chapter. For now, let's consider the primary message of angels—do they have anything to say to us today?

---

[1] As told by Sabra Scott.

[2] Graham, Angels, 3.

[3] McGee, J. Vernon, Through the Bible, Volume II, Thomas Nelson Publishers, 1982, 584.

CHAPTER NINE

The Message of Angels

Now that we've examined some of the overt ways angels can protect us and provide for our needs, we turn to the everyday ministry of angels: to deliver God's messages. The Greek word for angel (*angelos*) means "messenger." The same word *angelos* is sometimes used in Scripture to describe a human messenger. For example, in Revelation, the writer addresses "the angel of the church at…" and then names various ancient church locations such as Sardis or Ephesus). That reference is to the *human messenger* (pastor) of that church.

The Hebrew word for angel is *malachi* (similar to the prophet named Malachi), which also means "messenger." There are many examples in the Bible where angels function as God's "messenger boys." So, what message do these divine delivery boys carry from the throne room of heaven? Any message Gods gives them! Like a faithful postal employee, they merely deliver the message; they aren't responsible for its content.

However, when I carefully examined every instance in the Bible where an angel spoke, some interesting patterns emerged. I discovered several angelic messages or themes that appear over and over in the Word of God.

Afraid? Cheer Up!

The most common message angels give us is, "Cheer up!" although they may not use that term. The way angels usually express it is, "Do not be afraid" or, "Fear not."

For example, when angels appeared to Zechariah (Luke 1:13), to Mary (Luke 1:30), and to the shepherds on that first Christmas morning (Luke 2:10), their message was the same: "Do not be afraid."

When the angel appeared at the tomb of the Lord Jesus Christ and the women were shaking with fear, he told them, "Don't be alarmed" (Mark 16:6). I imagine most of us would need the same reassurance if we suddenly encountered an angelic being with a dazzling appearance. We'd be stunned, speechless, knees-knocking afraid! No wonder the first thing they usually do when they appear to people is calm their fears.

We also see angels delivering this message of encouragement in the Book of Acts. It traces the last recorded events of the Apostle Paul's life from a violent arrest to several mistrials. Finally, Paul is sent on board a ship bound for Rome. Once there, calamity on the open waters endangered all aboard. As the ship tossed in the middle of the storm, Paul spoke to everyone onboard, saying, "But now I urge you to keep up your courage, because not one of you will be lost; only the ship will be destroyed" (Acts 27:22).

How did Paul know this would happen? "Last night an angel of the God whose I am and whom I serve stood beside me" (Acts 27:23). In other words, an angel hand delivered this message.

When you belong to God and serve Him, He may send angels to speak to you. It may not be in a face-to-face meeting, as Paul experienced. However, God can get His message across in a number of ways.

The angel said to Paul, "Do not be afraid, Paul. You must stand trial before Caesar; and God has graciously given you the lives of all who sail with you" (v. 24). Paul continued, "So, keep up your courage, men, for I have faith in God that it will happen just as he told me. Nevertheless, we must run aground on some island" (vv. 25–26).

Do you need to "keep up your courage" in the face of some trial? What situation has you worried late at night? Are you afraid about what's happening in your family, in your marriage, in your portfolio? Do the events in our violence-laden world today frighten you? If you'll listen, I believe God's message to you could be, "Don't be afraid. Cheer up."

Angels in Disguise

The following story is but one of a number of accounts I've received in which people have had this positive message from an angel.

"On July 27, 2000, we had triplet grandbabies born to our daughter and her husband. They were healthy even though they were born prematurely, at 26 weeks. Each tiny baby weighed almost two pounds—Jackson and Christian, and a girl, Olivia. They were breathing on their own and for a week or so had no problems. Then Christian suddenly had a brain bleed and was put on a respirator.

"The triplets' doctor immediately called us to her office and informed us of the situation. Her options were: 'We can take Christian off the respirator and/or withhold food from him.' My 5' 9" daughter bolted out of her chair, slammed her hands down on the doctor's desk, and said very convincingly, 'That will never be an option! If I have to carry him around on a pillow his whole life, I'll do just that!'

"At that point, I left my daughter and son-in-law alone with the doctor and went to one of the waiting rooms. Each time I'd been there, it was so crowded I could hardly find a place to sit. This time, to my amazement, the room was empty. That never happened! I sat down and began crying and praying. I felt so alone. All of a sudden, I sensed someone in the room and saw a very large African-American lady standing in front of me.

"'Honey, are you all right?' she asked.

"I looked up and said, 'No, I'm not.'

"I asked her if she had a tissue. To my surprise, she pulled out a whole roll of paper towels and gave it to me.

"Then she asked me, 'Honey, what are you holding on to?' I told her I didn't understand, so she asked again, 'What are you holding on to? What are you crying about?'

"I couldn't answer her because I was crying so hard. She came over and took my right hand and said, 'You need to let go of whatever it is.'

"I said, 'You don't understand, it's my grandbaby.'

"About that time, another African-American lady came into the waiting room. She wore a "Jesus" baseball cap and a bright yellow T-shirt with "I Love Jesus" written on the front. She approached me and asked if she could pray for me. I nodded my head, so she sat down beside me and the first lady took my right hand.

"Next, a young girl came in and it was very apparent that she was a special needs child. For some reason, she came straight up to me and said, 'Your grandbaby is going to be okay. The Lord is going to take care of your grandbaby.' (How did she know?)

"Then, the second lady began to pray and the first lady opened my hand and said, 'Just let go.'

"The next thing I knew my daughter and son-in-law were standing in the waiting room, calling my name. I could tell they had been crying. I asked, 'Did you see two ladies in the hall?' They said, 'No. No one is here.' I ran out into the hall and looked both ways. I never saw them again, but I'll never forget their encouragement.

"Christian completely recovered from the hemorrhage. He is 100 percent normal, as are his brother and sister. They are now almost four years old and are as smart as any children I have ever seen—not to mention, the prettiest! I believe with all my heart that those ladies were sent from the Lord to minister to me in a way I never expected—and yes, maybe they were angels."[1]

Sleeping? Wake Up!

The second most common message angels give in the Bible is, "Wake up." Ladies, did you know you're never more like an angel than when you punch your husband in the ribs during church and say, "Wake up!"?

As you read the Bible, you'll be amazed at how many times an angel comes to wake somebody up. Elijah, for instance, was asleep when the angel came to him and said, "Wake up and eat." The story of Lot's angelic escape from Sodom and Gomorrah takes place in the wee hours of the night, and from the way the story reads, it appears that no one got any sleep that night. The angels didn't have to wake up Lot's family—they were there to make sure the family never went to bed on that fateful night.

Zechariah saw an angel in a dream. So did Joseph, who was the stepfather of the Lord Jesus Christ. For some reason, angels frequently appear at night and sometimes in dreams.

However, you should be very cautious about trying to find a message from God in every dream you have. Sometimes, weird dreams may be nothing more than the result of indigestion from eating cabbage and ice cream. Remember, however, that the Bible does say that sometimes people receive messages from angels in dreams.

I've received letters in which people have written about falling asleep while driving and narrowly escaping accidents. They recount that a voice suddenly woke them in time to avoid a collision. It's amazing how many times an angel will come to us while we're asleep, with the urgent message, "Wake up, wake up."

Peter Encounters an Angel

We find a good example of this celestial "wake-up" call in Acts 12, regarding Peter's arrest and imprisonment for preaching the gospel.

> The night before Herod was to bring him to trial, Peter was sleeping between two soldiers, bound with two chains, and sentries stood guard at the entrance. Suddenly an angel of the Lord appeared and a light shone in the cell. He struck Peter on the side and woke him up. "Quick, get up!" he said, and the chains fell off Peter's wrists (vv.6–7).

Peter was obviously astonished by what was taking place. The angel's sudden appearance apparently so confused him that the angel had to tell him everything to do, step by step!

> Then the angel said to him, "Put on your clothes and sandals." And Peter did so. "Wrap your cloak around you and follow me," the angel told him. Peter followed him out of the prison, but he had no idea that what the angel was doing was really happening; he thought he was seeing a vision. They passed the first and second guards and came to the iron gate leading to the city. It opened for them by itself, and they went through it. When they had walked the length of one street, suddenly the angel left him (vv.8–10).

Peter's wake-up call came just in time, on the eve of his execution. While Herod had planned to squelch the spread of the Christian message through the underhanded arrests and murders of its high-profile supporters, God had another plan in mind. An angel appeared with the stealth of a special forces operative, stealing Peter away right under Herod's nose, and carrying him to safety and the waiting arms of a gathering of believers we see huddled in prayer for Peter's return.

In Acts 12:5 we read, "So Peter was kept in prison, but the church was earnestly praying to God for him." The key word in this sentence is the conjunction, "but." Peter was in a seemingly hopeless situation in earthly terms; *but* prayer was already at work. This passage seems to indicate a direct correlation between the activity of angels and the prayers of God's people.

The Importance of Prayer

What lesson can we learn from this correlation? Whenever you awake suddenly, pause for a moment and listen. I have no trouble going to sleep. I usually sleep soundly throughout the night and wake up very refreshed. But, like most of you, there are times when I wake up suddenly in the middle of the night. For years, I didn't know how to account for it.

Since I've done this study of angels, when I awaken suddenly without apparent cause, I always listen. I respond, "I'm awake now, God. Did you awaken me for some reason? Did you send an angel to wake me, to tell me to pray for somebody?" Almost every time, God lays someone on my heart for whom I should pray. I listen and I start praying, sometimes for as long as an hour. I use that time to listen to God and to pray for someone's needs.

May I suggest to those who wake up suddenly in the middle of the night not to be frustrated or waste that sleepless time worrying or afraid. Instead, I challenge you to pray. Consider it a divine appointment between you and the Lord. So often we spend our "awake" time worrying, filling our minds with bad thoughts of the worst that could happen.

Jesus taught us we ought always to pray and not give up (Luke 1:18). The NASB says, "Pray and do not lose heart."

The Greek word translated "give up" is *enkenkao*. It literally means to "be filled with bad thoughts."

Worry is like water. It begins as a trickle of doubt that creeps into our mind. If it isn't averted, it soon becomes a stream of fear, that creates a pool of paranoia, that overflows into a river of distress, that develops into a torrent of tension. And before you know it, the flood of worry has carved a Grand Canyon of anxiety in your mind!

Philippians 4:6–7, words penned by a man sitting in a damp, dark, depressing dungeon, are a vivid reminder to us: "Don't fret or worry. Instead of worrying, pray. Let petitions and praises shape your worry into prayers, letting God know your concerns. Before you know it, a sense of God's wholeness, everything coming together for good, will come and settle you down" (*The Message*).

When you face a challenging circumstance that keeps you up at night, you have two choices. You can lose heart and let worrisome thoughts control your mind; or you can pray about it. What's the better choice? You should pray and not worry, because the God of the Bible loves you and cares for you.

The rest of the story concerning Peter's miraculous escape from prison teaches us one more principle about the relationship between angelic activity and the prayers of God's people—the importance of expecting God to act. The believers who gathered to pray for Peter's safety fervently expected God to come through for him. They didn't know how He would do it, but they were confident He would, or they wouldn't have been together on their knees. However, their response to Peter's release teaches us an important lesson.

After the angel left him on the street, bewildered but free, Peter finally realized what had happened. "Then Peter came to himself and said, 'Now I know without a doubt that the Lord sent his angel and rescued me from Herod's clutches and from everything the Jewish people were anticipating'" (Acts 12:11). He then made his way to the prayer meeting at the home of Mary.

> Peter knocked at the outer entrance, and a servant girl named Rhoda came to answer the door. When she recognized Peter's voice, she was so overjoyed she ran back without opening it and exclaimed, "Peter is at the door!" (vv.13–14).

She didn't believe her eyes, and neither did the believers. The very thing they had prayed would happen had occurred—but it just seemed too good to be true. Thankfully, despite their initial shock, they didn't keep Peter waiting long.

We must *expect* God to answer our prayers. Even if the answer isn't exactly what we wanted to hear, we can trust it's for our good and His glory. It goes back to what we've been discussing about the way one views life and reality. If we've closed our mind to the presence of angels and the God-ordained spiritual dimension of our lives, it doesn't render those things any less real. It simply makes us unaware of what's really happening. In the same way, if we doubt we'll receive an answer to prayer, chances are we won't.

James adds a powerful warning about letting doubt creep into your prayers. He writes, "But when he asks, he must believe and not doubt, because he who doubts is like a wave of the sea, blown and tossed by the wind. That man should not think he will receive anything from the Lord" (James 1:6–7).

Compare that to the positive promise we find in 1 John 5:14–15: "This is the confidence we have in approaching God: that if we ask anything according to his will, he hears us. And if we know that he hears us–whatever we ask–we know that we have what we asked of him."

The difference is learning to pay positively, without doubting. Sadly, many Christians pray, but they really don't expect an answer. I heard about a children's Sunday school teacher who encouraged the class to pray for missionaries and even write them a personal letter. The teacher explained that missionaries are very busy and wouldn't have time to send a reply to every child, so they shouldn't expect to hear back from them.

One little boy wrote this letter: "Dear Mr. Smith, I am praying for you. I'm not expecting an answer." Are you like that? You pray, but you aren't really expecting an answer? If you're sensitive to God prompting you to pray, don't forget to pray expectantly, patiently waiting on His timing for an answer.

Also, it's acceptable to pray for angelic protection. We don't pray to angels, but we do pray for God to dispatch angels to protect us, to protect our loved ones, and to deliver us. In the Book of Acts, believers were praying for Peter to be delivered, and the angels came in response to their prayers.

I pray for my wife and daughters to be protected by angels. Every time my family and I travel, I pray for God to send His angels to protect us.

Behind the Scenes

Hopefully, you're beginning to see that behind our everyday lives is a backdrop of spiritual warfare—supernatural battles between good and evil. I'm not one to over-spiritualize everything that happens throughout a person's day. However, I do believe applying a spiritual perspective to everyday events helps to put life in the right context.

For example, envision your home as a spiritual battleground. What take place within those four walls are either losses or victories, spiritually speaking. Your spiritual enemy, the devil, delights when spouses erupt in an argument or children disobey.

Spiritual warfare isn't a term reserved for major events, such as a battle with cancer. It takes place more often than we may realize, in daily experiences common to us all at home, at work and at school.

As we've also discussed, however, this spiritual warfare is invisible. If we could open our eyes to see the spiritual realities all around us, we'd be shocked at the intensity and the scope of warfare between angels and demons. Fortunately, God has sent his ministering spirits, the angels, to help us in specific ways—namely, to provide for our needs and protect us from harm.

Angels Eager to Help

In Daniel 10, we gain a glimpse of this invisible warfare and the angels' eagerness to come to our aid. Daniel reported that he'd been praying about a specific scenario for twenty-one days without an answer. However, an angel came to him and shared the reason why his prayers were seemingly unanswered for a period.

The angel said, "...your words were heard, and I am come in response to them. But the prince of the Persian kingdom resisted me twenty-one days. Then Michael, one of the chief princes, came to help me, because I was detained there with the King of Persia" (Daniel 10:12–13).

Many have taken this to mean that the devil was resisting the fervent prayers of Daniel. Michael, the archangel, and the angel speaking to Daniel, fought against the "prince" (a demon) for the prayer to be answered.

When we're on our knees praying, we're involved in the thrust of spiritual warfare. God's angels are available to respond to the prayers of God's people. When are angels available to us? Whenever we're in need.

What Angels Do Not Do

Now that you know what angels spend the majority of their time doing, you may be surprised to discover what God has ordained for them *not* to do. There are certain spiritually important activities we *do not* have scriptural evidence of angels or any other created being ever doing. Angels may wish they could participate, but, in fact, God has left the responsibility to us alone.

---

[1] As told by Annell Barron.

CHAPTER TEN

What Angels Wish

One night, I was out visiting homes in an area around our church. Another church member and I went to the home of a recent visitor to our church, but no one was there. As we were walking away, I heard an audible voice as clearly as I've ever heard say, "Go to the house next door."

My friend didn't hear anything. I don't often do this, but I went to the house next door, not knowing who lived there.

We knocked on the door and an elderly man opened it. We told him we were visiting from the church and asked if we could speak to him. He was very kind and invited us inside. We accepted, and began to share the gospel with him.

Our conversation went so smoothly it was unbelievable. The man was hungry to learn how he could know Christ. We explained what the Bible says about knowing Christ and what it takes to be saved. He prayed and invited Jesus to come into his heart and take control of his life.

After awhile, he said to us, "I want to tell you something. Last week I went to the doctor. He examined me, X-rayed my chest and told me he found a spot on my lungs. I was so afraid. That night, I lay in bed and I looked at the ceiling and said, "God, I don't even know who you are or where you are, but I'm in trouble. Would you send somebody to tell me how I can get right?"

Isn't that amazing? We weren't even going to that house. We were leaving the house next door, and it was as if God directed us to go to the man who had prayed that someone would come.

The third most common message angels proclaim is to "speak up." Sometimes, God uses an angel to tell us another common message of angels, "Speak up!" As we'll soon learn in this chapter, angels wish for the opportunities we have to share Christ with others. Why? Because they're so enamored with Him and quick to fulfill His command, they couldn't help but shout it from the rooftops. But it's God, not angels, commanding us to speak up on His behalf and share the gospel story.

Can Others Hear You?

Luke, in Acts 5:17–20, recorded the events surrounding the apostles' imprisonment:

> Then the high priest and all his associates, who were members of the party of the Sadducees, were filled with jealousy. They arrested the apostles and put them in the public jail. But during the night an angel of the Lord opened the doors of the jail and brought them out. "Go, stand in the temple courts," he said, "and tell the people the full message of this new life."

Notice that the angel came during the night. This is when it seems angels do much of their work. In the middle of the night an angel came, woke up the apostles, escorted them from prison and delivered a message. He directed and exhorted them to tell people the full truth about Jesus Christ, and to hold nothing back.

As you study the Word of God, you'll find that many times angels have told people to go and speak up for Christ. Angels don't preach the gospel to lost people because they don't understand it the way humans do. I suspect the reason angels never deliver a message about salvation is because they don't even comprehend what salvation is. They've never been lost, spiritually speaking; thus, they've never been saved.

In 1 Peter 1:12, Peter is discussing salvation. He writes, "Even angels long to look into these things." Angels don't understand grace or faith, but they long to know more about their beloved Lord and how He demonstrated His love for us. They're that devoted to Him.

Angels don't comprehend the salvation experience from a personal point of view, so they haven't been assigned to communicate the gospel message. Only we have that personal perspective, because the gospel is for us, not angels. Although angels may wish they had our job, it's not their responsibility.

There Is No Plan B

It would be easier, though, wouldn't it, if God would just send evangelistic angels throughout the world to preach the gospel. But He doesn't do that. We're the only ones commissioned to do so.

There's a story about a fictional conversation between an angel and God in heaven one day. Looking down at the mass of people inhabiting the earth, the angel says plaintively, "Who will tell all those people about the love of Christ?" God says in reply, "My people will tell the world—that's how everyone will come to know the truth." The angel thinks about this for a moment and says, "What if they don't tell anyone? What's Plan B?" God looks at the angel and says simply, "There is no Plan B."

Sometimes angels urgently whisper in our spiritual ears: "Speak a word for the Lord Jesus Christ." Have you ever felt

God was trying to tell you to say something about Him to a co-worker or friend? That's what the angel told Peter, John and the others. What angels *wish* they could do—herald the gospel from sea to sea—we're actually *supposed* to do. There's no other plan for the world to know how to be saved.

Why Not Just Send an Angel?

In Acts 8:26; we read that God sent an angel to deliver a message to Philip. "Now an angel of the Lord said to Philip, 'Go south to the road—the desert road—that goes down from Jerusalem to Gaza.'" There, the angel explained, Philip would find an Ethiopian man who was seeking the truth.

At that very moment, the man was reading Scripture (the book of Isaiah, to be exact) as he was being chauffeured around in his chariot. The problem was, he didn't understand what he was reading. God used this angel to arrange a divine rendezvous between a seeker and a witness. As a result, the man accepted Christ and was baptized.

Have you ever wondered why God didn't just send the angel to preach to the Ethiopian? Why go to the trouble of enlisting Philip to go? Angels deliver many messages, but nowhere in the Bible do angels ever deliver evangelistic messages to lost people. We can only conclude that angels, given a choice, may wish they could do so, but that's not in their job description.

In contrast to the angels' enthusiasm for the gospel, some Christians wish God had arranged it so that they wouldn't have to share their faith. Wouldn't it be simpler if we could just become Christians, get our ticket to heaven and not worry about talking to anybody else about Jesus? For some people, the thought of sharing Christ with a co-worker, a friend or, worse yet, a family member is terrifying. *What if they reject me? What if they think I'm a religious nut? What if...*The excuses go on and on. So, many remain silent.

Some would prefer that God send His angels to tell the good news, but that's not His plan. God sends angels to deliver messages to His own children, but He gives us both the privilege and the responsibility of delivering the message of salvation to those who are spiritually lost.

Do you really care about those who don't know Jesus personally? In and of ourselves, we don't care about lost people. But God can give us a wonderful gift—giving us the same concern He has for lost people. Paul said in Romans 9:1, "I speak the truth *in Christ.*"

That's the key. Paul was in Christ and Christ was in Paul. The more you are in Christ and the more Christ is in you, the more you'll be concerned about people who don't know Jesus, because Jesus was concerned about people who didn't have a relationship with God.

In Luke 19:10, Jesus said, "For the Son of Man came to seek and to save what was lost." The more you're filled with Jesus and the love of Jesus, the more you'll be concerned about people who are without Christ. The more you're full of yourself, the less you'll be concerned and the more you'll stay silent. We could leave it to God or the angels to do it—but, remember, there is no Plan B.

Seek a Seeker

We see this message proceeding in two different directions. First, a Christian may be directed to speak to a nonbeliever. Let's pick up the details of the story about Philip and the Ethiopian.

> Then Philip ran up to the chariot and heard the man reading Isaiah the prophet. "Do you understand what you are reading?" Philip asked.
>
> "How can I," he said, "unless someone explains it to me?" So, he invited Philip to come up and sit with him.

> The eunuch was reading this passage of Scripture: "He was led like a sheep to the slaughter, and as a lamb before the shearer is silent, so he did not open his mouth. In his humiliation he was deprived of justice. Who can speak of his descendants? For his life was taken from the earth.
>
> The eunuch asked Philip, "Tell me, please, who is the prophet talking about, himself or someone else?" Then Philip began with that very passage of Scripture and told him the good news about Jesus. (Acts 8:30–35)

Have you ever looked at someone and wondered if that person knows Jesus Christ? Did you hear a voice that seemed to say to you, "Why don't you speak to that person about Christ?" I've heard that voice many times. Whether it's the Holy Spirit or a ministering spirit, it doesn't matter. Many times God is trying to direct us to speak to people about Jesus Christ.

You say, "Well, I don't believe in talking to other people about religion. That's a private matter." If all we were talking about was religion, I'd want to keep it private too, but we're talking about the most life-changing relationship a person can ever have. Once you understand why that is, you can't stay silent about it.

Look for a Christian

Sometimes the delivery method of an angel's message works in reverse. A nonbeliever may be directed by an angel to seek a Christian. It's amazing to observe how God can orchestrate a rendezvous between two people.

Acts 10:1 states, "At Caesarea there was a man named Cornelius, a centurion in what was known as the Italian Regiment. He and all his family were devout and God-fearing; he gave generously to those in need and prayed to God regularly." That's the description of a good man, but he was not a Christian. He wasn't saved yet. Even today, some people think that surely they're Christians because they're devout, fear God, give money, and pray. You can do all those things and still not be born again.

The story continues in verses 3–5:

> One day at about three in the afternoon he had a vision. He distinctly saw an angel of God, who came to him and said, "Cornelius!"
>
> Cornelius stared at him in fear, "What is it, Lord?" he asked.
>
> The angel answered, "Your prayers and gifts to the poor have come up as a memorial offering before God. Now send men to Joppa to bring back a man named Simon who is called Peter."

Do you see what's happening? In the first story, the angel directed Philip, a Christian, to go and speak to the Ethiopian, a nonbeliever. But, in this incident an angel directed a lost person, Cornelius, to go seek a Christian. He was directed to send for a Christian to come and share the truth with him.

Why didn't that angel who appeared to Cornelius just rattle off the four spiritual laws or at least give the guy a gospel tract? Why didn't the angel give that message? It wasn't his responsibility.

The Bible says, "How, then, can they call on the one they have not believed in? And how can they believe in the one of whom they have not heard? And how can they hear without someone preaching to them? And how can they preach unless they are sent? As it is written, 'How beautiful are the feet of those who bring good news.'" (Romans 10:14–15). Sharing the heavenly message is a uniquely human responsibility.

"You Are Needed"

We've had incidents in our lives for which we didn't know the causes. If we look back, we might realize we'd heard the voice of an angel. Another time in my life, it seemed as if an angel told me to speak to someone. I was a senior at Samford University in Birmingham, Alabama. My wife, Cindy, had already graduated from Auburn University and was teaching school, while I was finishing my last year of college. Each weekend, we drove to Prattville, Alabama, where I was Minister of Youth at the First Baptist Church.

One afternoon, we were driving down the highway in front of the university and, as we were approaching a main intersection, we were stopped by backed-up traffic. About a quarter of a mile in the distance, we saw all kinds of emergency vehicles: fire trucks, ambulances and police cars.

It's against my nature to stop and gawk at a wreck. I usually try to stay out of the way and let trained personnel care for the injured. I don't stop at the site of an accident unless I happen to be the first person there. However, as we stopped on that particular afternoon, a voice seemed to say to me, "Go up there. You are needed." I couldn't even see what was happening at the scene.

Let me pause here to give you a little background information. Cindy and I had hosted a weekly Bible study in our apartment. Some of the young people from our church who were students at Samford would come and bring their friends. One of the girls brought a freshman friend named Sandy. We became acquainted with her as she continued coming to Bible study.

After hearing the voice, I got out of my car and walked toward the accident. As I approached a bridge, I saw a car had gone off the road, missed the bridge and landed in the water, upside down. Water was covering everything except the very bottom of the car and the wheels. I wondered how anybody could get out of that car alive.

I looked over at the fire truck and saw a weeping girl seated on the step. She had a blanket wrapped around her, and she was talking with a fireman. She and I looked at each other, and immediately I realized it was Sandy. The moment she saw me and recognized a friendly face, she jumped up and rushed over to me.

The fireman said, "Do you know her?"

I said, "Yes, sir. Is there anything I can do to help?"

The emergency medical technician had already checked Sandy and found nothing physically wrong.

She was immensely relieved that a friend was there to give her comfort and strength. I was needed. I had never heard that kind of voice before. It seemed God knew I was there and that Sandy needed a friend.

That's really not the most amazing thing about that incident. Sandy said that when she missed the bridge and her car was falling into the water, she felt hands under her arms, pulling her out of the car.

The astounding thing was that neither her hair nor her clothes were wet. To this day, she doesn't know how she got out of that submerged car, but she believes God miraculously delivered her.

You may say, "Well, that's just coincidence, hysteria at a time of trauma." Yet, Sandy believes God rescued her, and I believe God gave me a message to go there and help her. Sometimes angels say, "Speak up." If you're listening, an angel may direct you to speak to people throughout your day—to encourage them, to pray with them or to share Christ with them.

Preoccupied with Praise

Angels most often deliver messages to "Cheer up," to "Wake up," and to "Speak up." However, they also deliver one more common message, to "Lift up—lift up the name of Jesus!" Angels are preoccupied with praising God. Psalm

148:2 contains this call to praise, "Praise him, all his angels, praise him, all his heavenly hosts." The phrase in the Bible, "heavenly hosts," is a term to describe the angelic armies. Angels participate with all of creation to praise God.

The book of Revelation has more than sixty references to angels. There are more references to angels in Revelation than any book except Psalms. Isn't it interesting that the two books of the Bible that speak more about angels are Psalms and Revelation–where there's more praise and more worship than in any other books in the Bible?

We're told in Revelation 4:8 that four angelic creatures (with different faces and six wings each) are in heaven to praise God; they stay at the throne of God and praise him night and day. But, there are other angels who shuttle back and forth to heaven. Sometimes they're in the presence of the Father and sometimes they're here on earth.

I believe those angels praise God when they're in His presence as well as when they're here. As we learned in a previous chapter, angels, as far as we know, don't sing their praises to God; rather, they speak and continually chant it.

Next to the privilege of sharing the gospel, I imagine that high on an angel's wish list is one we often take for granted—singing God a new song, lifting our voices in praise and bursting into a melody of praise. Angels long to praise God continually—and maybe they even wish we more intimately knew what they know firsthand from the throne room of heaven. That He is awesome and holy. He is worthy of praise.

Angels Among Us

When we gather to worship and praise the Lord, the angels are present with us. There's something about an atmosphere of praise and worship that's conducive to the activity and the presence of angels. If God could open our spiritual eyes as we're worshipping and praising the Lord, I believe we could see God's angels encamped all around, praising God with us.

I heard a story about a young Christian woman who recalled a similar experience. As a girl at a church youth camp, she was lying awake in her cabin one night, reflecting on the day's events and all the Lord's blessings. She was silently praying and praising God in her heart when suddenly the camper next to her bed sat straight up in the dark and cried out, "I just saw an angel sitting on your bunk!"

While the young girl never saw the angel on her bed, she smiled to herself as she went to sleep that night, certain that a welcome angel had slipped in to join her in praising the Father.

In Revelation, chapters 4 and 5, we read that one day, when we're in heaven, we'll gather around the throne of the Lamb and praise Him, saying, "Worthy is the Lamb who was slain." Angels have known the character of Jesus since they were created. One day, they'll join with us in this mighty doxology of tribute to Jesus. And the Bible clearly says that day of angels may be in our future sooner than we expect.

CHAPTER ELEVEN

Angels in Our Future

Years ago, as I was writing some notes for this book on angels, I received a call that one of our dearest church members had died suddenly. The night before, he had routinely put on his pajamas and fallen asleep. Only he woke up with Jesus. As his wife and I spoke that morning, we talked about how, sometime during the night, the angels had come and visited Wayne and carried his soul and spirit into heaven.

In Luke 16, Jesus tells another fascinating truth about angels. He relates the story of an unnamed rich man and a righteous beggar named Lazarus. In Luke 16:22, He said, "The time came when the beggar died and the angels carried him to Abraham's side."

It's comforting to know that angels are with us throughout our lives—even to the end. God sends his "escort angels" to ensure that our souls are seen safely into heaven when we transfer our address from this world to the next one.

That's another reason why a Christian never has to fear death. The presence of angels reminds us we're never separated from the love of God—even at death. "For I am convinced that neither death nor life, neither angels nor demons, neither the present nor the future, nor any powers, neither height nor depth, nor anything else in all creation, will be able to separate us from the love of God that is in Christ Jesus our Lord" (Romans 8:38–39).

Angels at Our Death

While the Bible teaches that angels attend to us at our death, many cultures and traditions personify death itself in the form of a spirit being, but not necessarily an angel. For example, in European folklore, a common character called the Grim Reaper shows up to deliver the bad news that it's someone's time to die. In Greek and Roman mythology, the gods Thanatos and Mors, respectively, represented "Death" (as if it were a person) and certain aspects of death.

You may have heard the term "angel of death" assigned to the angel at the first Passover in Exodus 12, but that exact reference is not used in the Bible. Extra-biblical Jewish Literature originated the term, "angel of death." When referring to this event, the Apostle Paul designates this angel as "the destroying angel" (1 Corinthians 10:10). Even though this term isn't explicitly used in the Bible, God does employ His angels on a number of occasions from the Old Testament through Revelation to exact the judgment of death (see 2 Samuel 24:16 and Isaiah 37:36).

The Bible, however, makes an important distinction about death. It's portrayed as an event; it's not personified or spiritualized. In contrast to literary sources, biblical angels are there to attend to believers at their death and escort their souls to heaven, where Jesus will be waiting. You can be sure that if you're a believer, Jesus will receive your spirit when you die—not some personification of death like the Grim Reaper.

It can be an unsettling thought to contemplate our own mortality, but the Bible doesn't mince words when it comes to death and dying. "Man is destined to die once, and after that to face judgment" (Hebrews 9:27). It could be that, for some of us, the first and only encounter we have with angels in our lives comes at the end of our lives.

When Jesus Comes

Some of you reading these pages may never experience death. Believers who are still alive when Jesus comes to rapture the Church and take all the Christians throughout the earth with Him to heaven won't need angels to escort them to paradise. Jesus Himself will do it.

The return of Jesus to Planet Earth is taught throughout the New Testament. Christian groups may disagree about the details of His return, but anyone who reads Scripture cannot deny the fact of His Second Coming and that angels will accompany His return.

Jesus says, in Matthew 13:41–42, "The Son of Man will send out his angels, and they will weed out of the kingdom everything that causes sin and all who do evil. They will throw them into the fiery furnace, where there will be weeping and gnashing of teeth."

Although angels will accompany Jesus at His return, it's obvious they don't know when this fantastic event will occur. He taught, "No one knows about that day or hour, not even the angels in heaven, nor the Son, but only the Father" (Matthew 24:36). Today, there are many self-proclaimed prophets who claim to know more than the angels (or even Jesus) because they're predicting when Jesus will return.

Whenever I read or hear of someone who has predicted the date of Christ's return, I know immediately that he's wrong—Jesus made it clear that even the angels don't know the day or the hour. As one of my friends likes to say, "When it comes to the Second Coming, I'm not on the scheduling committee, I'm on the welcoming committee!"

Angels and the Second Coming

Where is Jesus today? Over two thousand years ago, He died, was buried and, after three days and three nights, God the Father restored Him to life. For forty days, He remained on the earth, appearing to more than five hundred witnesses, but at the end of that forty-day period, he ascended back into heaven. And that's where He rules and reigns today.

Not only did the disciples and other believers witness Jesus ascend into heaven. Observe what the angels said at that time. In Acts 1:10–11, we're told:

> They [meaning, the disciples] were looking intently up into the sky as he was going, when suddenly two men dressed in white stood beside them. "Men of Galilee," they said, "why do you stand here looking into the sky? This same Jesus, who has been taken from you into heaven, will come back in the same way you have seen him go into heaven."

The disciples stood there and watched Jesus ascend into the sky. I can imagine they looked at Him for as long as they could, like people watching a space shuttle, trying to keep their eyes on it until it becomes a tiny speck in the sky. Finally, these two angels drew away their attention with the startling announcement that Jesus was going to return—in the same way they had seen Him leave this earth.

Jesus had this to say about His Second Coming:

> At that time the sign of the Son of Man will appear in the sky, and all the nations of the earth will mourn. They will see the Son of Man coming on the clouds of the sky, with power and great glory. And he will send his angels with a loud trumpet call, and they will gather his elect from the four winds, from one end of the heavens to the other. (Matthew 24:30–31)

You say you've never seen an angel? The Bible says that one day every eye will watch Him come back to the earth in the glorious company of angels. However, as spectacular as seeing a host of angels at once might be, I guarantee that everyone's attention will be squarely transfixed on Jesus Himself, the Son of God, not His holy angels. After His triumphant return, what other roles will angels play in our future?

Angels During the Tribulation

Again, many Christians disagree about the details and the order of many of the events at the end times, but we all agree on one thing—Jesus is returning. After Jesus raptures the Church, I believe Scripture teaches that there'll be a seven-year period of terrible tribulation and crisis on the earth, led by a one-world ruler whom the Bible calls the Antichrist. (We don't know who he is now.)

God will use the assistance of His mightiest angels to pour out terrible judgments upon the earth. God's judgment poured out on earth is pictured symbolically in Revelation by three series of sevens. Seven seals on a book are opened, and the seventh seal leads into seven trumpets, each one describing a cataclysmic event. A series of angels are seen blowing trumpets announcing judgment. Each angel announces a judgment to come that is even more devastating than the one before it.

Although angels play a role throughout the series of judgments, we see, with the blast of the sixth trumpet, that a small, special division of angels are released.

The sixth angel blew his trumpet, and I heard a voice coming from the horns of the golden altar that is before God. It said to the sixth angel who had the trumpet, 'Release the four angels who are bound at the great river Euphrates.' And the four angels who had been kept ready for this very hour and day and month and year were released to kill a third of mankind. (Revelation 9:13–15)

These are special angels created seemingly for no other reason than for this. There are not quite six billion people on earth right now. In this single judgment, angels are responsible for the destruction of one third of the world's population. It boggles the imagination, but this is exactly what the apostle John saw.

Angels Will Accomplish His Judgment

If you want to read a book in the Bible where angels are mentioned on nearly every page, consult Revelation. Here, angels are mentioned more than seventy times. Next to Psalms, this is more than in any other single book in the Bible.

In Matthew 13:24–30, 36–43, Jesus tells the story of the wheat and the weeds. In this story, the farmer planted wheat and was expecting a good crop. However, in the middle of the night an enemy entered the field and planted weeds among the wheat. As they began to grow, the strategy of the enemy became apparent.

Although the servants wanted to go out and pull up the weeds, the master cautioned them to wait. Instead, he insisted that the wheat and the weeds grow together and, at harvest time, they would be separated and the weeds would be burned.

In Matthew 13:37–42, Jesus explains the role of angels in judgment by unpacking the truths in this parable. "The one who sowed the good seed is the Son of Man. The field is the world, and the good seed stands for the sons of the kingdom. The weeds are the sons of the evil one, and the enemy who sows them is the devil. The harvest is the end of the age, and the harvesters are angels."

The judge is the Lord Jesus Christ, but you might say His bailiffs are His angels. He will send them forth to execute His judgment. All the unrighteous who have not surrendered to Jesus as the Lord of their lives will be gathered up by the angels and judgment will come upon their lives. As a pastor, I don't delight in writing about God's judgment, but I know it's an essential truth in God's Word.

The God of the Bible is more loving and compassionate than any human being. His patience is unfathomable. His heart's desire is not that any should perish, but that all would repent of their sin and accept His free offer to live forever in heaven with Him. However, because God is also a holy God who cannot tolerate unrighteousness, He must judge sin.

Remember, in Matthew 25, Jesus says hell was prepared for the devil and his angels. God didn't prepare hell for you or your loved ones. He longs for everyone to be saved. I hope you've trusted the Lord Jesus Christ with your heart so that, when you witness the angels who will play a part in the future judgment, you won't be in that number who'll have judgment executed upon them.

Angels at Satan's Demise

Not only will the angels execute judgment upon the earth, but an angel will be the one who executes judgment upon the chief fallen angel, Satan himself. A whole army of angels will not be needed to overthrow the villain—not a battalion, not a legion, but one single angel will accomplish the overthrow of Satan. Read how the Bible describes this event:

> And I saw an angel coming down out of heaven, having the key to the Abyss and holding in his hand a great chain. He seized the dragon, that ancient serpent, who is the devil, or Satan, and bound him for a thousand years. He threw him into the Abyss, and locked and sealed it over him, to keep him from deceiving the nations any more until the thousand years were ended. After that, he must be set free for a short time. (Revelation 20:1–3)

This powerful angel, armed with a chain, is going to throttle Satan, put him in the bottom of his pit, and shut him up for a thousand years. The devil will have a brief furlough from his prison, but then he will be cast back in for eternity.

You ask, "What does all of this mean?" For one thing, it shows that angelic activity serves as bookends in the Bible. From the angels stationed outside the Garden of Eden to those accompanying Jesus' return, angels are central to the Bible's teaching.

Jesus experienced the ministry of angels and emphasized angels throughout His teaching—especially about what will happen at the end times. I don't just *think* angels are going to be in our future—Jesus said they *would* be.

Joy in the Presence of Angels

In Luke 12:8–9, Jesus also emphasized the *witness* of angels: "I tell you, whoever acknowledges me before men, the Son of Man will also acknowledge him before the angels of God. But he who disowns me before men will be disowned before the angels of God."

This truth contains both an encouragement and a warning. Whenever we publicly confess that Jesus is our Lord, He is faithful to claim us as His child before the angels. However, if we refuse to accept Him as our Lord, He will publicly disown us before the angels. Have you confessed Jesus as the Lord of your life? If you have, you can be sure the angels heard the good news from Jesus Himself.

In Luke 15, Jesus tells three consecutive stories about something that's lost, then is found. He's really teaching us what God is like. He first tells of a shepherd who leaves his sheep to search for one lost lamb. This speaks of how God's love searches for us. Next, He tells of a woman who has ten coins but loses one, and turns her house upside down to find it. She doesn't give up until she does. This speaks of God's stubborn never-give-up kind of love.

Jesus completes the trilogy by telling of a father whose rebellious son breaks his heart, leaves town and then humbly returns. This speaks of God's suffering love—a love that aches for us when we go our own way.

In each of these stories, there's a parallel scene of joy when the sheep, the silver and the son are found. Jesus says, "In the same way, I tell you, there is rejoicing in the presence of the angels of God over one sinner who repents" (Luke 15:10).

I've often heard this verse slightly misquoted. Some people say, "the angels rejoice over one sinner who repents." While that may be true, that's not what Jesus said. Look at it again. He said there's joy "*in the presence of angels*" when one sinner repents. Does the joy come from the angels themselves or from the One in whose presence they are?

The language seems to indicate that Someone else is rejoicing and the angels witness and benefit from the rejoicing. When you understand this, it's a bonus blessing. When you surrendered your heart and life to Christ, God rejoiced over your return to Him. The angels were privy to the moment that brought a smile to the Father's face.

You may have had many big decisions in your life—where to live, what job to take, what person to marry. You may have also received many accolades and awards for your achievements. However, none of these significant decisions and events has been cause for heavenly celebration. In other words, none of them, no matter how important to you, counted for eternity. The only human decision that brings rejoicing in heaven, and catches the attention of angels, is the decision to accept Christ.

If you've yet to surrender your life to Jesus Christ, a grand angelic celebration may still be in your future. There's still time to make this pivotal, life-altering decision, while you're still alive and Jesus has yet to return.

For the Skeptics

After reading about the ministry of these supernatural beings and their central role in the Bible, you may still be a little skeptical. You may be wondering if you can believe everything you've read. The Bible is neither logical nor illogical—it's supralogical. It exceeds human understanding.

You can't always figure out God's activity in a scientific test tube with observable, repeatable results. You can't decipher on a computer what He does. You may have become so skeptical that when you read the evidence of heaven on earth you say, "I'm not too sure about that." Remember, there will always be a mystery about God's ways that we cannot unravel. He says, "As the heavens are higher than the earth, so are my ways higher than your ways and my thoughts than your thoughts" (Isaiah 55:9).

Learning to recognize and appreciate signs of heaven on earth doesn't mean you check your brains at the door. It's not for the intellectually inferior. Nor is it for those who consider themselves intellectually superior. Jesus said you must become as a little child to understand the things of God.

Having made it this far in this book, maybe it's time you drop your intellectual questioning and say, "By faith, I believe in God and I believe what God's Word says." You have to be willing to say in childlike faith, "God, I don't understand You, and I don't understand all Your ways, but I trust You. I believe You, not only with my life, but with my eternity. Open my heart to understand what you want me to learn about the spiritual reality You created."

Have you ever encountered an angel? Don't be too quick to say, "No." Hebrews 1:14 tells us God had sent His ministering spirits to serve those who are heirs of salvation. God may have sent a stranger to you and you simply didn't recognize him. Be thankful that God loves you and, when you pray, "Heaven, help us," remember He may be dispatching His angels in answer to your prayer. Chances are, an angel is watching over you even at this moment.